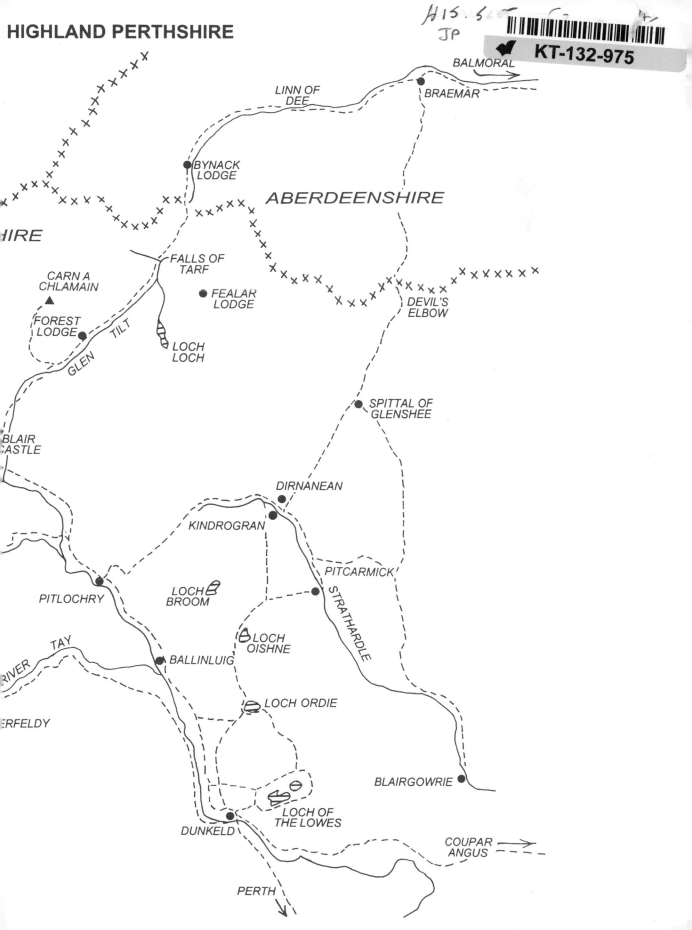

HIGHLAND PERTHSHIRE

BALMORAL

BRAEMAR

LINN OF DEE

BYNACK LODGE

ABERDEENSHIRE

...SHIRE

FALLS OF TARF

CARN A CHLAMAIN

FEALAR LODGE

DEVIL'S ELBOW

FOREST LODGE

GLEN TILT

LOCH LOCH

SPITTAL OF GLENSHEE

BLAIR CASTLE

DIRNANEAN

KINDROGRAN

PITCARMICK

PITLOCHRY

LOCH BROOM

STRATHARDLE

RIVER TAY

LOCH OISHNE

BALLINLUIG

...ERFELDY

LOCH ORDIE

BLAIRGOWRIE

LOCH OF THE LOWES

DUNKELD

COUPAR ANGUS

PERTH

Queen Victoria's

SCOTTISH DIARIES

Queen Victoria and Duchess Anne were together on each of the Queen's six visits to Highland Perthshire

Queen Victoria's
SCOTTISH DIARIES
. . . her dream days

John Kerr

. . . As for the great Queen herself,
these dream days in Atholl and Breadalbane
were a perfume that sweetened her life
to the very end.

Dr T. Crouther Gordon
PERTHSHIRE ADVERTISER
18 April 1951

BROCKHAMPTON PRESS
LONDON

This book is dedicated to my children,
son-in-law and daughter-in-law:
Julia, Rosalind and Simon, Charles and Gerani.
Also to my grandchildren: Camilla, Samuel,
Sabine and Joshua.

First published by Eric Dobby Publishing,
12 Warnford Road, Orpington, Kent BR6 6LW

This edition published 1998 by Brockhampton Press,
a member of Hodder Headline PLC Group

British Library Cataloguing in Publication data available upon request
from the British Library.

ISBN 1 86019 3862

Typeset in Perpetua by Blackpool Typesetting Services Ltd, Blackpool
Book design Mark Blackadder
Printed in Great Britain by The Bath Press, Bath

Contents

Foreword

With a present-day Range Rover, complete with all modern equipment, it would be a daunting task to follow in the footsteps of Queen Victoria. Some of the journeys she made which are described in this book are quite remarkable; for instance, in October 1861 she rode sixty-nine miles in one day, and much of that was on tracks which were ill-marked. In fact, on her 1865 trip to Perthshire the coachman lost his way, on a cold, wet and dark October night causing her and her party to arrive for their stay with Duchess Anne several hours late – and the only person who was totally unmoved by this was the Queen. You cannot help admiring her endurance and disregard of comfort when you read through this selection of her travels. I really do pity her entourage.

Atholl
BLAIR CASTLE
24 June 1991

Acknowledgements

The Duke of Atholl has assisted and encouraged me with all my research and writings for over twenty-five years and once again I thank him most sincerely for the facility to research this project in the Charter Room at Blair Castle; also for allowing me to photograph maps, drawings, letters and old photographs as well as in the castle itself. I am most grateful to Mrs Jane Anderson, the archivist, for all her help in locating much of this material.

I would like to thank the Hon Mrs Jane Roberts and her team in the Print Room at Windsor Castle and Miss Frances Dimond in the Royal Archives for their assistance with paintings, drawings and photographs from the Royal Collection. John Murray (Publishers) have given me permission to reprint a few extracts from *Charlotte Canning* by Virginia Surtees. Alasdair Steven very generously lent me illustrations from *Queen Victoria in Scotland* to reproduce for this book, while the staff of the Local History Department in the Sandeman Library, Perth, helped me to find copies of local newspapers which covered the Queen's visits.

Sir George and Lady Nairn and their keeper at Pitcarmick, Mr John Manning and his farm manager at Dirnanean and Mr Alastair Lavery at Kindrogan all gave me useful information and allowed me to cross their land while researching Queen Victoria's travels of 1865 and 1866.

Finally, the help of my wife Patricia has been constant and invaluable throughout, not only in assisting with the research but also in deciphering my handwriting and then typing the manuscript.

Illustrations on pages 63 and 101, Windsor Castle, Royal Library © Her Majesty the Queen and on pages 124 and 161, Windsor Castle, Royal Archives © Her Majesty the Queen. © Virginia Surtees 1975. All other pictures by the author.

Introduction

Queen Victoria more than anyone else, popularised the Scottish Highlands and through news-paper accounts and the later publication of her diaries, the beauties and attractions of the country were revealed to the world. Official visits by royalty to Scotland were a rarity at that time: no state visit had taken place since the coronation of Charles II in 1651, so Queen Victoria and Prince Albert's visit in 1842 – after a gap of nearly 200 years – was a momentous event. The Queen's uncle, King George IV, had come to Edinburgh in 1822, but he was remembered mainly for his appetite for money, food and women and newspaper editors were quick to remind their readers of the 'costly and ridiculous fooleries' which had epitomised his visit and hoped that 1842 would be a more dignified and sober affair.

Although she travelled extensively throughout Scotland during her reign, from the Border hills to the west coast and north to Dunrobin and Loch Maree, Queen Victoria returned frequently to Atholl and Breadalbane. These two ancient areas between them make up most of Highland Perthshire where mountains, moorlands, forests, lochs, tumbling streams and mighty rivers combine to form a dramatic landscape – spacious and unspoilt – some of the most spectacular scenery in Europe. The Comitatus or Earldom of Atholl, descended through the ancient Celtic Earls whose heartland centred on Blair Castle, home first for the Stewart Earls and, after 1629, the Murrays, ancestors of the present Duke. The once vast lands of Breadalbane, stretching from Loch Tay to the Atlantic, were from the fifteenth century the stronghold of the Campbells of Glenorchy, who built Balloch Castle in the following century, replacing it with Taymouth at the end of the eighteenth.

Queen Victoria kept a diary from the age of thirteen until a few days before her death in 1901, in which she made daily entries of the events in her life. Here she recorded scenes of imperial splendour, described journeys in minute detail and vividly recollected the people she met and places she visited. After the death of Prince Albert in 1861 she determined on pub-lishing some of these memories and Arthur Helps, Clerk to the Privy Council, edited the diaries into book form. *Leaves from the Journal of our Life in the Highlands* she dedicated 'To the dear memory of him who made the life of the writer bright and happy these simple records are lovingly and gratefully inscribed.' The book was an immediate bestseller, somewhat to the dismay of her children and the royal household, who on the one hand disliked the public exposure of their private lives and on the other resented the apparent elevation of the Queen's Highland servants.

In 1884 a second volume, *More Leaves from the Journal of a Life in the Highlands* was published, based on her diaries between 1862 and 1882. This time the dedication was 'To My Loyal Highlanders and especially to the Memory of my Devoted Personal Attendant and Faithful Friend John Brown', who had recently died. The Queen received great assistance in the editing of this second volume from Miss Amelia Murray MacGregor, cousin of the 6th Duke of Atholl and long time friend and companion of his wife, Duchess Anne.

Between 1842 and 1866 Queen Victoria made six journeys to the Atholl and Breadalbane area and in this book extracts from her diaries have been used as a thread to guide the reader through Highland Perthshire, to visualise the places as she saw them and meet the people she encountered. The diary extracts are highlighted throughout the book and a great many of the references to the people and places in them are explained and often illustrated.

Charlotte Canning, Lady of the Bedchamber, accompanied the Queen to Blair Castle in 1844 and she too kept a meticulous diary, adding a different view of events, and some extracts from her account appear in chapter 2. Amelia MacGregor wrote a comprehensive, detailed narrative of the Queen's visit to Dunkeld in 1865 and of the first two days of the 1866 visit, which details minutely all the places she went to and the people she met. Extracts from this, as yet unpublished, manuscript appear in chapter 5 and briefly in chapter 6.

The book is illustrated throughout with many old photographs which give a contemporary glimpse of the Highlands in Queen Victoria's time and allow us to see how places have changed. There are photographs of the Queen and Prince Albert, of members of their family and of some of the royal household who accompanied them, together with some of the people she met. The 6th Duke and Duchess of Atholl, neighbouring lairds, the Atholl Highlanders, stalkers and keepers are all represented. Old maps are used to illustrate the routes of her journeys and contemporary pictures again help to interpret her descriptions of the beautiful Highland Perthshire countryside.

Letters from the Queen and from some of her children have been included, often in full, and these, along with newspaper extracts and eyewitness accounts, provide a close feel of events. All the eccentricities of the spelling of Gaelic names have been preserved in quotations, while the modern Ordnance Survey spellings have been adhered to elsewhere. This seems the only possible compromise, though it does lead to apparent inconsistencies.

Queen Victoria's visits to Highland Perthshire began in 1842 on a very high note with the formal ceremonial reception in Dunkeld, moving on to the lavish magnificence of Taymouth Castle. In contrast, the 1844 stay in Blair Castle, though still on a fairly grand scale, was of a totally different nature – it was a private visit with no trappings of state, a time for relaxation away from pomp and ceremony and a chance to meet the ordinary people of the country and to be attended by 'loyal Highlanders', whom the Queen came to trust more and more. Some of her most private and happy times were probably spent with Duchess Anne in her 'Cottage' in Dunkeld where 'all breathes peace and harmony and where it was so quiet and snug.' Here she stayed in a family home with the minimum of attendants and fuss. Such was the enthusiasm amongst the local people that cairns, inscribed plaques and simple stone monuments were erected to commemorate her visits. The good relationship between the Queen and Duchess Anne was further strengthened by the loss of their respective husbands within the space of two years, which created a firm bond between them. This becomes very apparent in the letters that the Queen and her children wrote to Duchess Anne: they all held their 'dearest Duchess' in great affection.

A great many changes have taken place in Highland Perthshire since Queen Victoria's visits, but the essential character of this beautiful land remains unchanged. In this book I have attempted to show the Highlands of Atholl and Breadalbane in words and pictures as they were in the last century, and have tried to demonstrate what attracted Queen Victoria to them repeatedly, making her time there her 'dream days'. It is a fitting tribute to her love of the area that this book should appear 150 years after Queen Victoria's first visit to her beloved Scottish Highlands.

Diary of Queen Victoria's Journeys in Highland Perthshire

Chapter 1

1842

Wednesday 7 September: First glimpse of the Highlands; ceremonial lunch in Dunkeld; travel to Taymouth Castle; formal dinner and fireworks.

Thursday 8 September: Prince Albert's first Scottish shoot; Queen Victoria visits the Dairy.

Friday 9 September: Walk in castle grounds; visit to Rock Lodge; grand ball.

Saturday 10 September: Tree planting ceremony; embarkation at Kenmore and row up Loch Tay to Auchmore near Killin.

Chapter 2

1844

Wednesday 11 September: Travel to Blair Castle with stop in Dunkeld; Prince Albert inspects the Atholl Highlanders.

Thursday 12 September: Walk in grounds to Diana's Grove and Old Blair; first visit to Glen Tilt.

Friday 13 September: Prince Albert's first shoot on the Atholl Estate.

Sunday 15 September: Church in Blair Atholl with escort of Atholl Highlanders.

Monday 16 September: Visit to the Falls of Bruar.

Tuesday 17 September: Walk in grounds to the Grotto overlooking the River Tilt and the York Cascade; drive to the Falls of Tummel.

Wednesday 18 September: Ride with Prince Albert to the top of Tulach Hill with only Sandy McAra as escort and guide.

Thursday 19 September: Deerstalking in Glen Tilt; sport spoiled by walkers in the glen, one of them the Episcopal minister.

Friday 20 September: Excursion to Allt Chrochaidh, ten miles up Glen Tilt.

Saturday 21 September: Full day's deerstalking in Glen Tilt.

Thursday 26 September: Drive through the Pass of Killiecrankie to Faskally, with the scene of the 1689 battle pointed out.

Friday 27 September: Servants' Dance in the Horn Hall; fire partially destroys the Factor's House, temporary home to Lord and Lady Glenlyon.

Tuesday 1 October: Departure from Blair Castle; stop at Dunkeld with a visit to the cathedral and the 'parent larches' and on to Dundee for embarkation to London.

Chapter 3

1861

Wednesday 9 October: Departure from Dalwhinnie through Drumochter and Glen Garry to Blair Castle for coffee; ride through and picnic in Glen Tilt on the way home to Balmoral.

Chapter 4

1863

Tuesday 15 September: By the new railway line to Blair Atholl station for a brief visit to the ailing 6th Duke in Blair Castle.

Chapter 5

1865

Monday 9 October: Departure from Balmoral by way of the Spittal of Glenshee to Pitcarmick in Strathardle; ride ponies over the hill to Loch Ordie; royal party lost for several hours in the rain and dark; late, but safe arrival in Dunkeld.

Tuesday 10 October: Drive to the Duchess's farm of St Colme's for tour and tea; visit to prize cows in dairy on way home.

Wednesday 11 October: Drive to Polney Loch, Cally Woods and the three Lochs of the Lowes; drive through Dunkeld to the Rumbling Bridge and the Hermitage.

Thursday 12 October: Walk in grounds to Dunkeld Cathedral and the American Garden; afternoon drive to Loch Ordie and a picnic.

Friday 13 October: Return to Balmoral via Ballinluig, Edradour and Moulin Moor with lunch stop at Kindrogan; ride over hill by Dirnanean to the Spittal of Glenshee.

Chapter 6

1866

Monday 1 October: Meet Duchess Anne at the Spittal of Glenshee and ride over the hill road to Kindrogan; drive after picnic tea to St Adamnan's Cottage, Dunkeld.

Tuesday 2 October: Drive to Cally Woods, Polney Loch and home by the River Tay; drive out after lunch to St Colme's.

Wednesday 3 October: Day drive of over seventy miles to Inver, Grandtully Castle, Aberfeldy, Taymouth Castle, Fearnan, Fortingall, Tummel Bridge, Queen's View and home via Pitlochry.

Thursday 4 October: Ride on pony through the Dunkeld grounds to the King's Seat and the otter hound kennels; drive after lunch, with a sketching stop of the castle in Clunie Loch; dance in the servants' hall.

Friday 5 October: Drive round the Lochs of the Lowes to Butterstone and on to Loch Ordie; picnic on the Braes of Tulliemet.

Saturday 6 October: Set off for Balmoral by carriage, changing to ponies at Loch Ordie and riding over the hill to Kindrogan; back to Balmoral by carriage after lunch.

CHAPTER ONE

1842
First Visit to the Highlands

DUNKELD AND TAYMOUTH,
WEDNESDAY 7 – SATURDAY 10 SEPTEMBER

The Perthshire Advertiser and Strathmore Journal was one of the first newspapers to tell the people of Highland Perthshire of the proposed official visit of Queen Victoria and Prince Albert to the area, in an article which appeared on 18 August 1842 under the heading:

Visit of Her Majesty to Scotland

Our readers will share the delight that we experience in learning that it is Her Majesty's intention to visit Scotland towards the end of the present month.

The people of Scotland are pre-eminently distinguished by a reverend regard for constituted authority, and we are quite assured that the first Magistrate of the Empire would receive from them a loyal and cordial welcome out of respect for the office itself even though the Character of the monarch did not present any peculiar claims to their esteem. But Queen Victoria is happily the possessor of virtues which give additional lustre to her station, and challenge the warmest love and veneration of her subjects. Wise, gentle and kind, exhibiting all the most winning characteristics of her sex, simple in her habits, generous and self-denying and of a most heroic courage, and beyond all, animated by an ever-present and anxious desire to promote the welfare and liberty of the people over whom she has been called to rule. To the loyalty which is entertained towards Her Majesty as the Sovereign, there is super-added a warmth of affection on account of her personal qualities and dispositions; and we are confident that her reception by the Scottish people of all ranks and classes will emphatically show that she does indeed dwell in their hearts.

The senseless pageantry by which it was sought to do honour to the visit of George IV to Scotland would be particularly out of place in the present circumstances of the country; and the sudden and unostentatious manner in which the Queen's purpose has been made known is another proof of her consideration and judgement as it shows that it is her wish that her progress through Scotland should be attended by as little pomp and circumstance as possible and with no unnecessary inconvenience to the people.

The Queen's first visit to the land of 'brown heather and shaggy wood' must indeed be marked by some demonstration worthy of and suitable to the occasion, but we trust that it will be of a character more becoming to the intelligence of the nation than the costly and ridiculous fooleries which signalised the visit of her uncle.

During the planning stages, Lord Glenlyon, in later life the 6th Duke of Atholl, learned of the Queen's proposed visit and immediately wrote to Sir Robert Peel, First Lord of the Treasury, offering to place his castle at Blair Atholl at her disposal. 'The Royal Forest of Athole has long been famous for red deer and should Her Majesty wish to see a drive of the forest after the ancient Highland fashion, every effort should be made to render it worthy of the occasion,' he wrote. Lord Glenlyon was well aware of Prince Albert's love of hunting, and offered this as an incentive to the royal couple to stay in Blair Castle. Sir Robert Peel replied within a few days informing Lord Glenlyon that the Queen 'is sensible of your kind consideration but fears that the time of Her Majesty's tour in Perthshire is so limited that Her Majesty will be unable on the present occasion to include a visit to Blair Castle in her arrangements.'

In his determination to entertain the royal party on their journey to Taymouth Castle, Lord Glenlyon offered 'the Park at Dunkeld' as a suitable place to stop for lunch and the Duke of Buccleuch, Lord Privy Seal, replied that 'Her Majesty and Prince Albert will accept your invitation to Dunkeld on their road to Taymouth from Scone on Wednesday 7th September.' Thus the scene was set for Queen Victoria's first royal occasion in the Highlands.

The royal party embarked at Woolwich on the Thames estuary on 29 August and landed at Granton near Edinburgh three days later. After spending a few days as guests of the Duke and Duchess of Buccleuch in Dalkeith House they headed north for Scone Palace near Perth, the family seat of Lord Mansfield. The next day, Wednesday 7 September, Queen Victoria had her first taste of the glories of Highland scenery as she approached Dunkeld, her route taking her around the foot of Birnam Hill, with glimpses of high mountains beyond. She recorded this moment in her diary:

First Glimpse of the Highlands

Wednesday September 7.

. . . We then changed horses at the New Inn at Auchtergaven. The Grampians came now distinctly into view; they are, indeed, a grand range of mountains.

To the left we saw Tullybugles, where it is said the Druids used to sacrifice to Bel; there are a few trees left on the top of the mountain.

To the left, but more immediately before us, we saw Birnam, where once stood Birnam Wood, so renowned in Macbeth. We passed a pretty shooting place of Sir W. Stewart's, called Rohallion, nearly at the foot of Birnam. To the right we saw the Stormont and Strathtay. Albert said, as we came along between the mountains, that to the right, where they were wooded, it was very like Thüringen, and on the left more like Switzerland. Murthly, to the right, which belongs to Sir W. Stewart, is in a very fine situation, with the Tay winding under the hill. This lovely scenery continues all along to Dunkeld. Lord Mansfield rode with us the whole way.

Of the Birnam Wood to which Queen Victoria refers in this entry, all that remains is the Birnam Oak, the last tree of the ancient oak forest which once covered the whole area and which was made famous by the witches' prophecy in Shakespeare's *Macbeth*:

Macbeth shall never vanquish'd be, until
Great Birnam Wood to high Dunsinane Hill
Shall come against him.

This relates to a battle reputedly fought in 1057, when soldiers of Prince Malcolm cut down branches in the wood and used them as camouflage as they attacked the king's fortress on Dunsinnan Hill, about twelve miles distant to the south. This ancient tree still stands beside the River Tay, and near it also grows the largest sycamore in the country, rising to a height of 100 ft (30 m). These are two of the most celebrated trees in Scotland, and have withstood the gales and floods for over a thousand years.

Preparations for the reception of the royal couple had been going on for several weeks, and many of the houses along the route were newly whitewashed. A bonfire was lit in celebration on the top of Birnam Hill the evening before and a young man, in apparent high spirits, rolled himself down the steep 100 ft (30 m) slope, sadly to be found unconscious at the bottom – he died soon afterwards.

Dunkeld

Just outside Dunkeld, before a triumphal arch, Lord Glenlyon's Highlanders, with halberds, met us, and formed our guard – a piper playing before us.

The last of the Birnam Oaks beside the River Tay, with the sycamore tree

This triumphal arch was erected at the southern end of Dunkeld Bridge. It was a magnificent gothic arch clothed in heather, topped with a floral crown and carrying the words 'Welcome to Athole'. A golden eagle was mounted on the left-hand side with a blackcock opposite, above two roe deer, one on each side of the road. The cavalcade stopped here at one o'clock and the Queen had her first sight of the Atholl Highlanders, forming a guard of honour from the Grenadier Company of two sergeants, a piper, a standard bearer and twenty rank and file, all of whom were over 6 ft in height and were commanded by Captain John Drummond of Megginch. The Highlanders were in full dress uniform bearing Lochaber axes, and were described as 'men of bone and sinew, showing they could have played with them as if they were reeds'. For the first time they were carrying a new regimental standard, consisting of the cross of St Andrew with the family arms surmounted by the words 'Athole Highlanders'.

A company of the 6th Dragoon Guards had escorted Queen Victoria as far as Dunkeld Bridge where they were relieved by the Atholl Highlanders, who then accompanied the royal party into the town. They proceeded slowly across the bridge to ringing cathedral bells, cheering crowds and a twenty-one-gun salute fired from a battery of cannon, many bearing the arms of the Isle of Man, on top of Stanley Hill – an artificial mound raised by James, 2nd Duke of Atholl, in 1730 as an extension to the grounds of Dunkeld House. On it were walks which zigzagged to the top, and it was planted with trees and shrubs. The battery was commanded by Captain Charles Hay of the Coldstream Guards.

Dunkeld Bridge, which consists of seven arches, two of them landlocked, was designed by Thomas Telford. Work started in 1805 and, after diverting the river during construction,

Dunkeld Bridge, completed in 1809

the bridge was completed in 1809. The Atholl family put up most of the money and, as they were anxious to recoup the losses incurred through the closure of the two ferries that served the town, a toll was levied on everyone and everything that passed: one person crossing the bridge paid ½d which included a return crossing on the same day; a horse and rider paid 1½d; a loaded cart 2d; a two-wheeled chaise 6d; a four-wheeled chaise 1/-; a coach 2/-; droves of oxen and cattle paid 1/8d per score; calves, lambs, hoggs, swine and goats 6d per score. Prior to all this, an Act of Parliament was required for permission to build the bridge:

> Whereas the two ferries upon the River Tay called Ferry of Invar and Lower or East Ferry are often liable to a great interruption and passage across said river and is sometimes attended with considerable danger owing to rapidity of said river, whereby communication between the Northern and Southern part is very much impeded. The said Duke of Atholl is empowered to erect a bridge of stone, iron or timber at or near said town of Dunkeld and to dig and make proper foundations in the said river.

There was much resentment amongst the local inhabitants about the imposition of the dues, and this grievance became more acute after the opening of the Perth–Inverness railway in 1856, as the station was situated across the river. This meant that every night the people of Dunkeld were almost under curfew after the toll man retired from his sentry box, and he had

George Augustus Murray, the second Lord Glenlyon   *Anne Home-Drummond*

to be summoned from his house each time the gates required to be opened. People from Birnam, the village which sprang up rapidly after the arrival of the railway, were unable to go to church in Dunkeld without this added expense. Feelings ran high in 1868 leading to the toll gates being wrecked and flung into the River Tay, with the result that a detachment of the 42nd Royal Highlanders was stationed in the town to quell the riots and restore order. It was not until 1879 that the problem was finally resolved, when tolls were abolished by an Act of Parliament and the big, white toll-gates were at last removed.

Once across the bridge the procession drove along Bridge Street, where many of the houses were decorated with crowns, flags and banners carrying the message 'Welcome to Dunkeld'. A splendid floral arch had been erected across the street by the premises of Mr Wallace, Coach-builder to Queen Victoria in Scotland. The Royal Standard of Scotland was raised both on the great tower of the cathedral and on the tower of the lodge leading to Dunkeld House.

> *Dunkeld is beautifully situated in a narrow valley, on the banks of the Tay. We drove in to where the Highlanders were all drawn up, in the midst of their encampments, and where a tent was prepared for us to lunch in. Poor Lord Glenlyon received us; but he had suddenly become totally blind, which is dreadful for*

Lord James Murray, brother of Lord Glenlyon

him. He was led about by his wife; it was very melancholy. His blindness was caused by over-fatigue. The Dowager Lady Glenlyon, the Mansfields, Kinnoulls, Buccleuchs, and many others, were there. We walked down the ranks of the Highlanders, and then partook of luncheon; . . .

On reaching the imposing gateway to Dunkeld House, Queen Victoria and Prince Albert were received by Lord and Lady Glenlyon. Lord Glenlyon was born George Augustus Murray in 1814, son of Lord James, the second son of the 4th Duke of Atholl. Lord James was specially created Lord Glenlyon to enable him to be received officially by King George IV during his state visit to Edinburgh in 1822, because his elder brother, John, who became 5th Duke in name only in 1830, had never fully regained his mental health after being invalided home from the army in Portugal in 1798. The first Lord Glenlyon therefore ran the Atholl Estate until his death in 1837, when George Augustus succeeded him as the 2nd Lord Glenlyon; following the death of his uncle in 1846, he became the 6th Duke of Atholl. In 1839 he married Anne, only daughter of Henry Home-Drummond of Blair Drummond. His affliction mentioned in the Queen's diary was a temporary blindness induced by paralysis of the optic nerve, caused by a heavy fall while out deerstalking and he never fully recovered the sight of his left eye.

Luncheon Festivities

A crowd of some 3,000 people had gathered in Dunkeld Park to greet the Queen, and a description of the scene appeared in *Memoirs of the Royal Progress in Scotland*:

> *The ground chosen as the theatre for this most exciting scene was that singularly beautiful lawn, stretching from within the ducal park gate of Dunkeld, westward beyond the site where the late Duke of Atholl commenced his princely palace, the walls of which are pretty well up. The particular spot selected for the encampment by Lord Glenlyon's brother, the Hon James Murray, Scots Fusilier Guards, to whose care all these military arrangements were confided, was that fine piece of lawn in front of the new house, with the right resting on Bishop's Hill.*

Lord Glenlyon had invited the lairds and landowners of the county to attend the gathering in full Highland dress and nearly 900 men, comprising the following, had marched into the camp the previous evening:

James McInroy of Lude with 1 piper and 30 men wearing the Atholl tartan with black jackets and belts.

William Dick Yr of Prestonfield with 27 men, from Urrard and Killiecrankie.

William Irvine from Pitlochry with 50 men from Faskally.

Henry Stewart of Balnakeilly with 30 men.

Muir and Samuel Fergusson of Middlehaugh with 15 men.

Patrick Small of Dirnanean and **Patrick Small Keir of Kindrogan** with 2 pipers and 50 men. (Patrick Small, who was presented to the Queen, was a man of immense size, completely belying his name).

Abercromby Dick from Tulliemet with 26 men.

Mr Sandeman of Bonskeid with 20 men.

The Duke of Leeds (Viscount Dunblane) with 1 piper and 10 men.

300 tenants from the Atholl Estate – 'stout yeomen'.

1 piper and 200 men from the Highland Society of Dunkeld.

400 members of the Masonic Lodges and Carpenters' Society.

40 mounted tenants from Strathord.

A further hundred Atholl Highlanders were also on parade, having been told a week earlier that they were 'required for three days' service to march to Dunkeld on Monday September 5th where they will remain on Tuesday 6th and to march back to Blair on Wednesday 7th where dinner will be provided for them at 1 o'clock after which they will be at liberty to return home.' Subsequently the date was changed and the Highlanders were asked to parade at Blair Castle a day later for the march to Dunkeld.

A tent city, made up of one large tent, fourteen marquees and twenty-four bell tents laid out in rows with military precision, formed a backcloth to the colourful gathering, the brilliant white canvas forming a vivid contrast with the bright green lawn and magnificent trees that surrounded the park. Tents had been ordered from Benjamin Edgington of 2 Duke Street, Southwark, London at a cost approaching £600, made up as follows:

A Marquee 96ft long 36ft wide with scarlet & white lining . . .	232- 0-0
6 Valises for . . . do . . .	4-10-0
A 4 breadth fancy Striped Marquee	16-16-0
Valise for . . . do . . .	10-6
A 4 Breadth Marquee . . .	16-16-0
Valise for . . . do . . .	10-6
4 Round Wall Tents £8.8.0 ea . . .	33-12-0
4 Valises for . . . do . . .	1-10-0
A 12ft Square Tent . . .	13-13-0
Flooring for Marquee 64ft by 20ft . . .	45- 0-0
A 5 Yard Royal Standard . . .	7-10-0
A 5 yard Union Jack . . .	3-15-0
	376- 3-0

Brot on . . .   376- 3-0

On Hire

2 Marquees . . . 22 × 14 . . .	16-16-0
2 Round Wall Tents . . .	8- 8-0
6 Flanders Tents . . .	18-18-0
6 Captains . . . do . . .	18-18-0

Superintending the erection
 of the Marquees & Tents –
Mens time – coach hire etc
Travelling expenses etc . . .   59-10-0

£498-13-0

On Hire at Lord Glenlyon's Dunkeld

A Pavilion 64ft by 20ft
with scarlet & white lining
throughout, a boarded floor
covered with crimson cloth,
looking glass, drapery
rosettes, etc etc.
A retiring Tent for Her Majesty
adjoining the pavilion.

Superintending the erection
Mens time & expenses etc . . .   £89-14-0

Sir Thomas Dick Lauder described the royal pavilion in his account of the Royal Progress:

> THE QUEEN'S PAVILION (which was pitched facing the cathedral, so as to afford Her Majesty a fine prospect of the lawn), was beautiful. The outside was striped blue and white, and the lining broad scarlet and white. It was floored with timber covered with crimson cloth. By a new plan of mounting it upon shears, all tent poles were dispensed with, so that it thus formed one great, perfectly uninterrupted and extremely handsome saloon 64ft long by 20ft wide. The interior was dressed out with flowers and flags, and a magnificent mirror, ten feet by six, was placed at one end. As the weather was delightful the canvas forming the walls of the tent on the southern side and western end, was not put up, so as to leave it quite open in these directions to the views and the air. Around it were placed a number of orange and other rare portable trees. There was a small retiring room for the Queen.

(The orange trees, some bearing fruit, were positioned in each corner of the Queen's Pavilion.)

Messrs Gunter & Co, 'Confectioners to Her Majesty and the Royal Family', were appointed to handle the catering and their principal assistant, Mr Rawlings, arrived in Dunkeld a few days beforehand, with a 'corps of cooks'. They took over the kitchen in the Brick Building, which had been cleared out for the purpose. This building, erected in 1769, formed part of the old Dunkeld House which has now completely disappeared.

Lunch for thirty-four people, including Lord Glenlyon's mother, the Dowager Lady Emily Glenlyon, was served in the Queen's Pavilion at two o'clock and cost £217 17s 0d.

The menu was made up as follows:

> *September 7* Luncheon (for Her Majesty and Suite at Dunkeld) consisting of White & Brown Soups, Hot & cold Entrees, Tongues Raised Pyes, Gallenteens, Hot & cold Chickens Aspics, Jellies, Creams Pastry, Pineapples, Ices, Cakes Biscuits, Bon Bons, etc etc
>
> The hire of Table, China, Linen, Silver, Glass, Gold Ornaments & every requisite including Mr Rawlings Cooks', Confectioners' and Attendants' time, travelling and Tavern Expenses for 17 Days to Scotland & back to London   182- 6-0
> 24 Bottles Champagne   8- 8-0

12	,,	Sherry	2-14-0
6	,,	Port	1- 7-0
6	,,	Claret	2- 2-0
1	,,	Maraschino	14-0
1	,,	Curaçoa	16-0
1	,,	Brandy	7-0
12	,,	Selzer Water	12-0

10 silk Banners with the Arms of his Lordship & those of Her Majesty painted in Colours and Gold		6- 0-0
	Carrd over	205- 6-0
1842	Brot over	205- 6-0
September 7	Paid Freight of Goods by the London Steamer from Dundee to London	9- 9-0
	Breakage of Glass & China	3- 2-0
		£217-17-0

A contemporary observer, writing in *Queen Victoria in Scotland*, detailed the lunchtime scene:

The dessert, elegant as it was abundant, consisted of queen pine-apples, grapes, peaches etc., currants en chemise, and ices in infinite variety. The pine-apples were served up on a splendid gold assiette monté, surrounded with grapes, and embellished with silken banners, with the national and Atholl arms. The service was of massive silver. Atholl brose was served to the Queen out of Neil Gow's glass, which is preserved by the Atholl family. It is of an ancient form, has the initials N.G. cut on the side, and holds nearly a quart. The wines and liquors were most choice, with iced Selzer waters, of which her Majesty generally partakes.

Atholl brose dates back to 1475. At this time, Sir John, 1st Stewart Earl of Atholl, led an expedition to crush a rebellion which had been mounted by John MacDonald, the Earl of Ross and Lord of the Isles. Tradition tells us that Sir John, hearing that his enemy was in the habit of drinking from a particular well, filled it with whisky and honey. This intoxicating mixture had such an effect on John MacDonald that, after drinking liberally from the well, he lay down, fell fast asleep and was easily captured. Nowadays, Atholl brose is a mixture of whisky, honey and sieved oatmeal.

After lunch . . .

the piper played and one of the Highlanders danced the 'sword dance'. (Two swords crossed are laid upon the ground, and the dancer has to dance across them without touching them.) Some of the others danced a reel.

The sword dance was performed by Charles Christie, who was born in Blair Atholl in 1816 and entered the service of Duchess Marjory, second wife of the 4th Duke, as a footman in Dunkeld in 1834. He performed the dance, 'displaying great alacrity and expertness in executing the steps'. His grandfather, John Christie, had been a carpenter at Blair Castle. During the Battle of Killiecrankie in 1689, Viscount Claverhouse, or 'Bonnie Dundee', was reputed to have been shot under his arm, but the breastplate in Blair Castle bears a hole through the centre. The story goes that this hole was made by John Christie under orders from the 4th Duke, who wished to give the breastplate a more warlike appearance! On the death of the 4th Duke, John was rewarded by receiving an annuity of £20.

Music for the sword dance was provided by John MacPherson, Pipe Major to the Atholl Highlanders since 1841. He worked as a hillman in Blair Atholl, had accompanied Lord Glenlyon to the Eglinton Tournament in 1839 and served the family for over forty years until he retired in 1880 through ill health. After the sword dance, two reels were performed by Sergeant George Stewart from Invervack; Corporal Duncan Menzies, Dalreoch; Piper Duncan Campbell, Blair Castle and Private Colin Fletcher from Balnaguard.

Departure from Dunkeld

At a quarter to four we left Dunkeld as we came, the Highland Guard marching with us till we reached the outside of the town.

The twenty men of the Grenadier Company of the Atholl Highlanders, led by their Captain, escorted the Queen back across Dunkeld Bridge where they were again met by the 6th Dragoon Guards, who continued on to Taymouth with the royal party.

Writing in her diary of the momentous day, Lady Glenlyon recorded that she:

Left Scone at 7 for Dunkeld, beautiful day. The Queen arrived about ½ past 1. Start for Taymouth at ½ past 3. Everything went off to a 'wish' without exception. Never forget!

Giving his views in a letter written the next day to Lord Glenlyon, the Duke of Buccleuch wrote:

In the hurry yesterday to get into the carriages I missed an opportunity of shaking you by the hand and congratulating you upon the success of your luncheon for the Queen. I was not quite an unconcerned spectator. I felt most anxious for you as an old friend and I take this first moment to tell you how well all your arrangements were made and how well the whole was conducted. The scene was beautiful and I am sure from what I have heard that the Queen and Albert were very much pleased and gratified. I write this in truth and necessity that you may know how others saw and appreciated what you had done.

Later, Queen Victoria wrote to Lady Glenlyon telling her that her 'whole Scotch tour delighted her', and she described in glowing terms her admiration for Dunkeld and the fine body of Highlanders.

The route chosen for the royal party to Taymouth followed the west bank of the River Tay and, once across Dunkeld Bridge, they turned right to Inver, a small village at the confluence of the wild and rocky River Braan with the more majestic Tay. Here a triumphal arch of flowers had been 'thrown' across the road from the west wing of Mr Pullar's inn. A number of Cambridge students were staying here with their tutor and they supplied the villagers with whisky and glasses, so that as the royal entourage passed by, the 240 inhabitants raised their glasses in unison and toasted the Queen, shouting, 'The Queen! God bless her!' Later they organised a ball in the inn and the night was spent in the 'utmost hilarity and harmony'.

> *The drive was quite beautiful all the way to Taymouth. The two biggest hills of the range on each side are (to the left, as you go on after leaving Dunkeld) Craig-y-Barns and (to the right, immediately above Dunkeld) Craigvinean. The Tay winds along beautifully, and the hills are richly wooded.*

The Queen was confused about the location of the two hills, as they are in fact the opposite way round.

It was the 3rd Duke of Atholl who conceived the idea 'that the rugged mountains round Dunkeld might be clothed with plantations, beautifying that place, with great after value.' The 'Planting Dukes' (2nd, 3rd and 4th) planted over fourteen million trees, covering an area of 10,000 acres. Only 250 years ago, before any form of organised planting had taken place, Craigvinean was a bare, heather-clad hillside with a little broom, gorse and juniper and a few rough pasture areas, called 'summer shielings', serving farmsteads lower down beside the Tay. One of the earliest attempts to plant trees on this hillside was in 1759 when James, the 2nd Duke, planted 700 larch intermixed with other trees below the summit of Craigvinean Hill. These trees were ornamental and were planted in rows like the spokes of a wheel, centring on a small loch near the river. The 3rd Duke continued planting on a considerable scale and was the first to depart from planting in straight lines – instead of creeping up a hillside with a few acres of trees in rows, he boldly took in the faces and heights of the hills around Dunkeld. He was the first person to plant larch commercially, and in 1767 3½ acres were planted below Craigvinean Hill. His son, 'Planter John', learned much from the mistakes of his father and grandfather, and introduced many improvements to methods of planting and general tree husbandry. At the time of Queen Victoria's visit well over a million trees, made up largely of larch, oak and Scots pine, were growing on Craigvinean.

Craig a Barns is part of the Atholl Estate. It is a sheer rock face, now often practised on by rock climbers and rises to almost 1,000ft (300m), dominating the landscape. It is made up of a range of rugged heights with crags, caves, streams and waterfalls, and helps to shield Dunkeld from the biting north winds. In Queen Victoria's day it was thickly covered with trees, which apparently sprang out of the rocks. The account of the sowing of these precipitous, rocky hills comes from *The Highland Tay* (1901) by the Rev Hugh MacMillan:

> *Originally they towered up to heaven bare and gaunt in their hoary nakedness; their sides being too precipitous to admit of being planted in the usual way. But Mr Napier,*

the famous engineer, while on a visit to the Duke of Atholl, suggested that the cannon in front of his host's residence might be loaded with tin canisters, filled with seeds of pine and spruce and larch, and then fired at the Craigs. This was done, when the canisters, striking the rocks, burst like shells and dispersed the seeds in the cracks and ledges, where they grew, and in course of time formed the vast billows of forest vegetation which have now submerged the highest points of the scenery.

Towards the end of his life, when the dream of his father had been realised, the sight of the forest scene brought about an emotional response in Planter John:

Drove up to Loch Ordie and home by the back of Craig-y-Barns, every way very much gratified with the growth of the larch and the spruce – a very fine, picturesque drive not to be equalled in Britain.

At Glenalbert, half a mile beyond Dalguise, a 'tasteful' triumphal arch had been hung across the road between two elm trees in honour of the Queen's visit, and at Milton of Kincraigie an arch carried the message, 'Welcome to Y'er Highland Glens', surmounted by a crown and the initials 'V.R.'.

We changed horses first at Balanagard (nine miles), to which place Captain Murray, Lord Glenlyon's brother, rode with us.

After travelling about ten miles, the horses were changed at the Balnaguard Inn. This change-house was built in 1790 and was described as 'a house lately built at Balnagaird on the Taymouth road which promises to be very comfortable for travellers'. Here a young girl from Logierait called Miss Jamieson, who worked at the inn, stepped forward and presented a nosegay of different types of heather to the Queen, which was graciously accepted and handed to Prince Albert, who fixed it in his jacket buttonhole. Because of Lord Glenlyon's illness his younger brother, Lord James Charles Plantagenet Murray, accompanied the royal party as far as the inn. Lord James was a captain in the Scots Fusilier Guards and it was he who had made all the arrangements for the Dunkeld reception.

The hills grew higher and higher, and Albert said it was very Swiss-looking in some parts. High ribbed mountains appeared in the distance, higher than any we have yet seen. This was near Aberfeldy (nine miles), which is charmingly situated and the mountains very lofty.

By this time the Queen and her party had entered Strathtay, where the Tay flows eastward in a graceful curve through one of the finest straths in Scotland, with richly cultivated and wooded slopes. Its numerous farms formed a patchwork, a 'quilted landscape', with fields and meadows stitched together in squares. The road passed below the 1,115ft (340m) hill called Castle Dow, meaning 'Black Castle', where lie the remains of a large Pictish hill fort surrounded by a circular stone enclosure. A number of nineteenth century cairns mark the summit above an area of natural woodland containing birch, Scots pine, yew and juniper.

The hills which Albert referred to as being 'very Swiss-looking' are the Farragon range, rising to 2,559ft (781m), with a long ridge stretching for several miles. A triumphal arch of heather, surmounted by a crown and carrying the message 'Welcome to Breadalbane', was erected about a mile east of Aberfeldy and informed the royal couple that they were now entering 'Campbell' country. A similar archway was passed through at the entrance to the town, where many of the houses had been whitewashed and decked with flowers and evergreens for the visit. Here the party again stopped to change horses and a crowd of 200 people gathered, each holding a brimming glass of whisky as they pledged the Queen's health and 'tossed off their bumpers'.

On the west side of the town the Tay is spanned by General Wade's finest bridge of five graceful arches, which was completed in 1735. After ten years of backbreaking labour, Wade and his 500 troops had constructed 240 miles of roads in Scotland through a country of rugged mountains where no true roads had existed before. This bridge on the military road from Stirling to Dalnacardoch and Inverness was the final link in the network of roads built to open up the Highlands and enable government troops to move quickly between their forts. The bridge took two years to build, was designed by William Adam and constructed from stone extracted from Bolfracks Quarry. It stands as proud and strong today as it did then and is a magnificent tribute to two brilliant men and the skills of their craftsmen.

North of the bridge the military road passes through Weem and goes by Castle Menzies, seat of the Menzies clan. It was extended and modified in 1571 and is a striking example of medieval architecture. A haunt of Mary Queen of Scots, Charles Edward Stuart stayed here for three nights on his way north to Culloden in 1746.

Taymouth Castle

At a quarter to six we reached Taymouth. At the gate a guard of Highlanders, Lord Breadalbane's men, met us. Taymouth lies in a valley surrounded by high, wooded hills; it is most beautiful. The house is a kind of castle, built of granite. The coup-d'oeil was indescribable.

The approach to Taymouth Castle from Aberfeldy is through natural woodland, with openings here and there to reveal the clear, sparkling Tay, cultivated fields and pastureland and dark blue mountains in the distance. A fine row of oak trees on the south side of the road was planted in 1842 on the recommendation of the Queen herself. The royal party arrived at the eastern gateway, an imposing gothic arch flanked by round, ivy-clad towers, through yet another heather-clad arch. From here a guard of honour of Breadalbane Highlanders escorted the Queen through policy woodlands, down the drive lined with hundreds of cheering people, to the castle.

This area had been dominated by the Campbells of Glenorchy since the fifteenth century and, though a cadet house, the Breadalbane Campbells became a mighty clan in their own right. By the time of the Queen's visit the 2nd Marquis was one of the largest landowners in the country, with some 400,000 acres stretching all the way to the west coast. As the eighteenth century drew to a close, the 4th Earl of Breadalbane pulled down his old stronghold of Balloch Castle, a mile from Loch Tay, because it was too small. The work of demolishing the central portion and east wing commenced in 1799 and the foundation stone of the new central block was laid two years later. This part of the new castle was completed within six years but the old west wing remained until 1838, when it was taken down and rebuilt in time for the Queen's visit.

> *There were a number of Lord Breadalbane's Highlanders, all in the Campbell tartan, drawn up in front of the house, with Lord Breadalbane himself in a Highland dress at their head, a few of Sir Neil Menzies' men (in the Menzies red and white tartan), a number of pipers playing, and a company of the 92nd Highlanders, also in kilts. The firing of the guns, the cheering of the great crowd, the picturesqueness of the dresses, the beauty of the surrounding country, with its rich background of wooded hills, altogether formed one of the finest scenes imaginable. It seemed as if a great chieftain in olden feudal times was receiving his sovereign. It was princely and romantic.*

The once-palatial residence of the 2nd Marquis of Breadalbane is situated about a mile east of Kenmore, in an extensive park renowned for its wide open spaces and magnificent trees. Here were some of the finest oaks, limes and chestnuts in Scotland. *The Illustrated London News* reported that preparations for the royal visit had been continuing for several weeks, with triumphal arches built at all the castle approaches and many tenants and visitors invited to attend, each bearing a quaich, with whisky being provided by the Marquis. 200 men from the Breadalbane Highlanders, who had been drilling for two hours earlier in the day, were stationed in front of the castle and sixty of these, each over 6ft tall and armed with Lochaber axe and shield, formed a guard of honour. Estate foresters and hillmen were in attendance dressed in simple plaids, along with a hundred men from the nearby Clan Menzies wearing their striking red and white tartan, which contrasted vividly with the dark green of the Breadalbane sett. They were led by their chief, Sir Neil Menzies, riding a white pony. The Menzies Company had two elegant silk banners, one displaying the chief's arms and the other with the message, 'God Save the Queen'.

On arriving at the castle entrance, the Queen and Prince Albert alighted from their carriage and the Royal Standard was run up in place of the Breadalbane flag. A royal salute was fired from batteries stationed near Kenmore and from the Fort immediately opposite the castle, where two 18-pounders and several 12-pounder guns thundered a royal welcome. The Fort was a small museum containing many examples of birds and animals found in the area, some of them very rare. Magnificent antlers and hunting trophies decorated the walls.

The royal couple were greeted by John Campbell, the Marquis, and the Marchioness. He looked every inch a chief in his Highland dress of velvet and tartan, covered with ornaments and jewels and wearing a bonnet sporting a heron's plume. He was the only son of the 1st Marquis and had succeeded his father in 1834 at the age of thirty-eight. He was educated at

Eton and had entered Parliament as MP for Okehampton at twenty-four. He was elected MP for Perthshire in 1832 and six years later was created a Knight of the Thistle. He married Eliza, eldest daughter of George Baillie of Jerviswood, in 1821.

> *Lord and Lady Breadalbane took us up stairs, the hall and stairs being lined with Highlanders. The Gothic staircase is of stone and very fine; the whole of the house is newly and exquisitely furnished. The drawing-room, especially, is splendid. Thence you go into a passage and library, which adjoins our private apartments. They showed us two sets of apartments, and we chose those which are on the right hand of the corridor or anteroom to the library.*

The entrance hall is particularly fine, resembling a cathedral transept as it soars 150ft (46m) to the roof. The grand staircase that ascends from it is of a gothic design, richly carved and decorated. Queen Victoria used the gallery and library as her private sitting rooms. The 70ft (21m) oak-panelled gallery leads to the library through a gothic-style carved oak door, where the ceiling is ornamented with carved mouldings and tracery and the walls were, at that time, lined with open bookcases containing a valuable collection of rare books. A concealed door, imitating one of the bookcases, led to the Queen's private apartments. The State bedroom was formerly known as the Chinese room because of its rich oriental wallcoverings.

Some idea of the sumptuous luxury of the castle is given by a contemporary description in *Queen Victoria in Scotland*:

> *The state bed is a beautiful specimen of workmanship and design, the frame of it being of the finest satin-wood, enriched with very highly finished carved and gilt mouldings and ornaments. At the corners are short, beautifully twisted pillars, entwined with wreaths of the Rose, Thistle, and Shamrock, and supporting marquises' coronets. The canopy, which is very lofty, is oval, splendidly carved and gilt, with depending pinnacles. The hangings are of the richest white satin, lined with peach-blossom silk, and trimmed with the richest deep gold bullion fringe, broad gold gimp and edging fringe, and finished with splendid gold rope and tassels. The teaster is of silver tissue, over which is laid beautiful antique perforated carving, richly gilt, having the imperial crown in the centre, with the royal cipher V.R., and from which diverge the coronets of all the various degrees. The foot-frame is stuffed, and covered with satin, tufted with gold rosettes and small tassels. The mattresses (for the Queen never makes use of feather-bed) are covered with the same satin, as are also the bolster and pillows. The counterpane is of the same satin and lining, and finished with beautiful gold edging fringe and gimp; the sheets are of the finest lawn, and the blankets of beautiful white cassimere, finished with white satin. In short the whole has a most splendid appearance, and at the same time is highly chaste and elegant.*

Prince Albert's sitting room next door was furnished with rich green silk damasks, ottomans and inlaid tables.

The drawing room occupies the greater part of the south side of the main block and extends to over 70ft (21m). The high ceiling is decorated with illuminations of fourteenth-century manuscripts on a gold background and the walls are covered with elaborate wood carvings picked out in cream and gold. Doors and woodwork are in satinwood and the chimney-piece is of pure white marble. The drawing room was completed in time for the Queen's visit, and an authority on stately homes maintained that nowhere in Scotland or England could rival it – he questioned whether there was anywhere in Europe to equal it.

Ceremonial Dinner

At eight we dined . . . The dining room is a fine room in Gothic style, and has never been dined in till this day. Our apartments are also inhabited for the first time.

The Baron's Hall, or dining room, is the principal room of the castle and is 60ft (18m) in length with a 30ft (9m) high ceiling divided into ninety sections by oak ribs, picked out in gold. In each of these is an armorial bearing of the Campbell cadet families since the twelfth century. A 20ft (6m) chimney dominates one end and stained glass windows light up the room from the west. Suits of armour, shields, halberds and two-handed swords were arranged around the walls along with paintings by old masters, while massive gothic lanterns were suspended from the ceiling.

A local reporter from *The Perthshire Advertiser* described the scene:

> The eye was dazzled by the glitter of gold and silver and gorgeous hangings and furniture. The service consisted of either gold or silver plate, largely the former. An immense gold candlebra stood in the centre of the table, weighty and massive and of elaborate workmanship. Numerous gold sconces containing wax candles were placed at intervals along the table and a splendid chandelier hung from the ceiling in the centre. Six tables groaned under a profusion of gold and silver plate and paintings of old masters adorned the walls.

Among the guests at dinner were: the Duke of Buccleuch, Lord Privy Seal, and his Duchess; the Duchess of Sutherland, Mistress of the Robes; the Marquis of Lorne, later the Duke of Argyll; the Earl of Aberdeen, Secretary of State for Foreign Affairs; the Earl of Liverpool, Lord Steward of the Household; the Earl of Morton, Lord in Waiting; Sir Robert Peel, First Lord of the Treasury; the Duchess of Norfolk, Lady in Waiting; the Hon Miss Paget, Maid of Honour in Waiting; Sir James Clark, Royal Physician; Major General Wemyss, Equerry in Waiting; Colonel Bouverie, Equerry in Waiting on Prince Albert and George Anson, Treasurer to Prince Albert.

The Firework Display

After dinner, the gardens were most splendidly illuminated – a whole chain of lamps along the railings, and on the ground was written in lamps, 'Welcome Victoria – Albert.'

A small fort, which is up in the woods, was illuminated, and bonfires were burning on the tops of the hills. I never saw anything so fairy-like. There were some pretty fireworks, and the whole ended by the Highlanders dancing reels, which they do to perfection, to the sound of the pipes, by torchlight, in front of the house. It had a wild and very gay effect.

At ten o'clock, as the autumn darkness gathered, a round from the Fort battery announced the start of the firework display and the royal diners moved to the window to view the spectacle of the castle and grounds illuminated by 50,000 lanterns. The words 'Welcome Victoria – Albert' were picked out in large letters by lanterns on the sloping lawn in front of the castle. A fine elm tree was lit up in a variegated pattern and an enormous crown, 15ft in height, with the letters 'V' and 'A' on each side, was illuminated on a knoll, also in front of the castle. The centrepiece of the display was round the Fort, 600ft up the hillside facing the castle. Here, thousands of lamps were lit to form the shape of a Turkish Pavilion, with crescents on each side and the Breadalbane standard crowning the centre. Other viewpoints, like the Star battery lower down and the Gamekeeper's Tower, were also highlighted and bonfires blazed on every hilltop around the castle.

The castle windows were brilliantly lit up to form a spectacular backdrop to the firework display, unequalled for splendour and extravagance by anything ever seen before, and one of the more spectacular set pieces slowly dissolved into a star with the letters 'V.A.'. Even more brilliant was a large triumphal arch, which suddenly appeared as a blaze of light and was crowned with the words 'Long live the Queen' in large letters, followed by a barrage of rockets, so that the Fort was suddenly enveloped in bright red light which slowly dissolved into green. This lit up the surrounding trees to breathtaking effect. The display lasted for nearly an hour and was followed by Highland dancing on three large raised platforms, lit by the glare from a hundred blazing torches, held aloft by Highlanders. Twelve pipers played *Gillie Callum* and the *Reel of Tullichan* as the sword dance was performed with 'agility and grace' and reels were danced with 'rare spirit'.

Taymouth, Thursday, September 8.

Albert went off at half past nine o'clock to shoot with Lord Breadalbane. . . . Albert returned at half past three. He had had excellent sport, and the trophies of it were spread out before the house – nineteen roe deer, several hares and pheasants, and three brace of grouse; there was also a capercailzie that had been wounded, and which I saw afterward – a magnificent large bird. Albert had been near Aberfeldy, and had to shoot and walk the whole way back, Lord Breadalbane himself beating, and 300 Highlanders out.

The Royal Hunt

Thursday morning was dull, with heavy rain and thick mist, and Albert, wearing a white hat, velvet shooting jacket, shepherd's tartan trews and light-coloured gaiters, set off for a morning's shoot on Bolfracks moor between Kenmore and Aberfeldy.

Writing of the sport in *The Illustrated London News*, William Scrope, the leading authority on the subject at the time, offered some advice, a little tongue in cheek, to Prince Albert:

> Your consummate deer-stalker should not only be able to run like an antelope, and breathe like the trade winds, but should also be enriched with various other undeniable qualifications. As, for instance, he should be able to run in a stooping position, at a greyhound pace, with his back parallel to the ground, and his face within an inch of it, for miles together. He should take a singular pleasure in threading the seams of a bog, or in gliding down a burn, ventre à terre, like that insinuating animal, the eel – accomplished he should be in skilfully squeezing his clothes after this operation, to make all comfortable. Strong and pliant in the ankle, he should most indubitably be; since in running down precipices, picturesquely adorned with sharp-edged, angular, vindictive stones, his feet will, unadvisedly, get into awkward cavities and curious positions; – thus if his legs are devoid of the faculty of breaking, so much the better, – he has an evident advantage over the fragile man. He should rejoice in wading through torrents, and be able to stand firmly on water-worn stones, unconscious of the action of the current; or if by fickle fortune the waves should be too powerful for him, when he loses his balance, and goes floating away on his back (for if he has any tact or sense of the picturesque, it is presumed he will fall backwards), he should raise his rifle aloft in the air, Marmion fashion, lest his powder should get wet, and his day's sport come suddenly to an end.

Meanwhile, up on the moor 300 men spread out to form a circle and drove the game towards Albert's position, and that day his 'bag' was 19 roe deer, 4½ brace of black cock, 3 brace of grouse, a wood pigeon, 12 hares and a brace of capercaillie. The capercaillie became extinct in Britain in the eighteenth century, due to a combination of dwindling pine forests and excessive hunting, but was successfully reintroduced to Perthshire in 1837, when the 2nd Marquis brought 28 birds from Sweden and a further 15 the following year. Prince Albert was the first to shoot capercaillie since their reintroduction.

Lord Glenlyon (left) with the Atholl Highlanders, commanded by Captain Drummond (right), preparing to meet the Queen at Dunkeld Bridge

Dunkeld, with the park on the right of the cathedral where the ceremonial lunch took place. Craigvinean Forest is in the background, with Craig a Barns to the right

Niel Gow's goblet from which the Queen had her first taste of Atholl brose

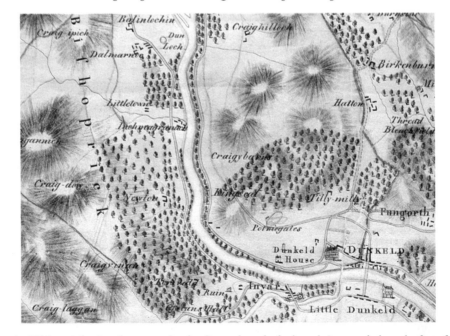

An 1815 map showing the route taken by the royal cavalcade through Inver and along the foot of Craigvinean on the west bank of the River Tay. Craig a Barns is on the right, and the road shown on that side of the river is the route taken by the Queen from Dunkeld to Blair Castle in 1844

John Murray, 3rd Duke of Atholl, 1764–74

'Planter John', 4th Duke of Atholl, 1774–1830

I walked out with the Duchess of Norfolk along a path overlooking the Tay, which is very clear, and ripples and foams over the stones, the high mountains forming such a rich background. We got up to the dairy, which is a kind of Swiss cottage, built of quartz, very clean and nice. From the top of it there is a very pretty view of Loch Tay. We returned home by the way we came. It rained the whole time, and very hard for a little while.

With Albert away shooting, the Queen went for a walk in the castle grounds, accompanied by the Duchess of Norfolk, her Lady in Waiting, and a liveried footman. They walked along the river bank, following the Berceau Walk, an avenue of tall lime trees extending for nearly a mile, and then up a slope to the Dairy. This sits on a knoll called Tom Mhor, overlooking the present-day golf course and is a striking building constructed of quartz from a rocky outcrop on a spur of Ben Lawers. It gleams in the sunshine and in Queen Victoria's day had a commanding view of Loch Tay, now obscured by trees.

The Queen entered by the kitchen door and was shown round by a dairymaid. Many of the rooms were floored with marble of various colours and the walls were inlaid with Dutch tiles. After watching butter being churned in a china vase, she turned the silver handle of the churn installed to commemorate her visit, drank some milk out of Rockingham china and tasted some oatcakes. *The Perthshire Advertiser* reported that when the dairymaid was asked what she thought of the Queen, she replied, 'She's as humble a leddy as I ever saw.'

We went out at five, with Lady Breadalbane and the Duchess of Sutherland; we saw part of Loch Tay and drove along the banks of the Tay under fine trees, and saw Lord Breadalbane's American buffaloes.

Kenmore

At five o'clock the royal party, in three carriages, headed for the Kenmore Gate, the imposing west entrance to the castle and entered the village to cheering crowds. Many of the houses had been whitewashed and decorated with heather and greenery. The inn keeper was determined to 'make hay while the sun shines' and, hearing that in Aberfeldy the price for accommodation was £1 per night, with a reduction to 15s each for two, decided to charge two guineas a night. Because of the scarcity of rooms in the village accommodation was at a premium, and half-a-guinea was charged for garret rooms and hay lofts. Some were prepared to pay 5s for a space on the floor!

Kenmore grew from a ferry station across the Tay in the sixteenth century and the first house was one built for the ferryman. Colin Campbell, 6th Earl of Glenorchy, who built Balloch Castle, wanted the church and ale house more conveniently situated on his side of the river and so in 1572 he built 'an hostelrie on the coble croft in Kenmore', the forerunner of the present hotel. Robert Burns visited Kenmore on 29 August 1787 and wrote these famous lines in pencil over the mantelpiece in the parlour of the inn:

Admiring Nature in her wildest grace,
These northern scenes with weary feet I trace,
O'er many a winding dale & painful steep,
The haunt of coveyed grouse & timid sheep,
My savage journey, curious I pursue,
Till famed Breadalbane opens to my view.
The meeting cliffs, each deep sunk glen divides,
The woods, wild scattered, clothe their ample sides,
Th' outstretching lake, embosomed 'mong the hills,
Th' eye with wonder and amazement fills,
The Tay meand'ring sweet in infant pride,
The palace, rising on its verdant side,
The lawns, wood-fringed in Nature's native taste,
The hillocks, dropt in Nature's careless haste,
Th' arches striding o'er the new-born stream
The village, glittering in the noontide beam.

The present church is a renovation of an earlier one built in 1579. Two hundred years later the 3rd Earl built the cottages on either side of the square to complete this very attractive village. At the Kenmore Bridge, a handsome five-arched construction completed in 1774, the Queen paused to admire the view up Loch Tay, beside another triumphal arch. From here the party turned right to enter the castle grounds beside the kitchen garden and recrossed the river by the Newhall bridge, a handsome iron structure erected by the 1st Marquis.

According to *The Illustrated London News* the royal party were entertained after dinner to a Scottish evening given by Mr Wilson, a celebrated singer. He sang a medley of songs requested by the Queen and these included, *Lochaber No More*; *The Lass of Gowrie*; *Pibroch of Donuil Dhu*; *Auld Robin Gray*; *Flowers of the Forest* and *Cam ye by Atholl*. The piano accompaniment was provided by Mr Lauder, director of the chorus at London's Theatre Royal in Drury Lane.

Friday, September 9.
Albert set off again after nine o'clock, to shoot . . . Albert returned at twenty
minutes to three, having had very hard work on the moors, wading up to his knees
in bogs every now and then, and had killed nine brace of grouse.

Albert's destination on this occasion was Drummond Hill to the north of Kenmore and, although it was still drizzling with rain, his tally in three hours was 9 brace of grouse, 6 alpine hares and a snipe. Drummond Hill forms an impressive backdrop to Taymouth Castle and stretches for several miles along the hillside beside the loch. Planting of trees started in the eighteenth century, and the 2nd Earl enclosed areas of the hillside in 1726 and 'sowed them thickly with trees'.

Soon after he left I walked out with the Duchess of Norfolk across the iron bridge,
and along a grass walk overhanging the Tay. Two of the Highland Guard (they were
stationed at almost every gate in the park) followed us, and it looked like olden times
to see them with their swords drawn.

We then walked to a lodge on the same road. A fat, good-humoured little woman, about forty years old, cut some flowers for each of us, and the Duchess gave her some money, saying, 'From her Majesty.' I never saw anyone more surprised than she was; she however came up to me, and said very warmly that my people were delighted to see me in Scotland. It came on to rain very heavily soon afterward, but we walked on. We saw a woman in the river, with her dress tucked up almost to her knees, washing potatoes. The rain ceased just as we came home, but it went on pouring frequently.

Once again the Queen, dressed this time in a Stewart tartan with red tartan shawl and light blue bonnet, and accompanied by her Lady in Waiting, walked in the grounds and covered a circuit of about three miles. They crossed the Tay by the Chinese Bridge at the back of the castle, headed towards Drummond Hill and soon arrived at the Rock Lodge. Here the gatekeeper, Mrs MacNaughton, a stout, active woman of about fifty, opened the gate and the Queen complimented her on her garden, especially the dahlias. The Duchess of Norfolk gave her money, saying it was from 'her Majesty', whereupon Mrs MacNaughton replied that 'the Queen's people are delighted to see the Queen in Scotland'. This encounter much pleased the Queen, who returned to the castle in high spirits.

We lunched; then we went to the drawing room, and saw from the window the Highlanders dancing reels; but unfortunately, it rained the whole time. There were nine pipers at the castle; sometimes one, and sometimes three played. They always played about breakfast-time, again during the morning at luncheon, and also whenever we went in and out; again before dinner, and during most of dinner-time. We both have become quite fond of the bagpipes.

Another exhibition of Highland dancing had been scheduled for three o'clock, but was delayed for an hour because of the weather. The Queen wore a white satin bonnet, tartan gown, crimson shawl and white scarf and watched the son of the Breadalbane piper, John MacKenzie, perform the sword dance 'with admirable precision and spirit'. A reporter noted that 'the exhibition was much better on this occasion'.

At a quarter past five we drove out with the Duchess of Buccleuch and the Duchess of Sutherland (poor Lady Breadalbane not being very well), Lord Breadalbane riding the whole time before us. We took a most beautiful drive, first of all along part of the lake and between the hills – such thorough mountain scenery – and with little huts, so low, so full of peat smoke, that one could hardly see anything for smoke. We saw Ben Lawers, which is said to be 4,000 feet high, very well; and further on, quite in the distance, Ben More – also the Glenlyon, and the River Lyon, and many fine glens. It was quite dark when we came home at half-past seven.

On this late afternoon drive the royal party passed through Kenmore and over the bridge along the north shore of Loch Tay as far as Fearnan, where they turned right to go up the hill to reach Glenlyon and Fortingall, completing a circuit round the back of Drummond Hill and arriving back at the castle as it was growing dark. (A full account of a similar journey made by the Queen in 1866 appears in chapter 6).

The Grand Ball

At eight we dined; Lord and Lady Ruthven and Lord and Lady Duncan dined here. After dinner came a number of people, about ninety, and there was a ball. It opened with a quadrille, which I danced with Lord Breadalbane, and Albert with the Duchess of Buccleuch. A number of reels were danced, which it was very amusing and pretty to see.

That evening the castle and grounds were once again illuminated by thousands of lanterns and a grand ball was held in the Banner Hall. Queen Victoria, wearing a white dress with a velvet scarf in Royal Stewart tartan and a brilliant tiara, 'the tout ensemble beautifully simple and chastely elegant', opened the ball by dancing a quadrille with the Marquis of Breadalbane, Albert partnering the Duchess of Buccleuch. Two hundred people, including two dukes, four duchesses, three marquises, two marchionesses, five earls and three countesses attended the ball, of whom fifty were presented to the Queen. Country dances and reels followed and while the Queen retired just after midnight, dancing continued into the early hours.

Saturday, September 10.
We walked to the dairy and back – a fine bright morning; the weather the two preceding days had been very unfortunate. I drove a little way with Lady Breadalbane, the others walking, and then got out and each of us planted two trees, a fir and an oak.

Saturday morning was bright and clear and, following another walk to the Dairy, the Queen and Albert visited the flower garden east of the castle, where they both planted a Scotch fir and an oak tree. A special spade with an oak shaft and handle covered in crimson cloth was used for the ceremony.

John Alston, inventor of an 'embossed alphabet', the forerunner of Braille, was a guest at the ceremony and presented the Queen with a beautiful cassock which had been made in his home for the blind in Glasgow.

Embarkation

We got in again, and drove with the whole party down to the lake, where we embarked. Lady Breadalbane, the Duchess of Sutherland, and Lady Elizabeth went by land, but all the others went in boats. With us were Lord Breadalbane, and the Duchess of Norfolk and Duchess of Buccleuch; and two pipers sat on the bow and

> *played very often. I have since been reading in the Lady of the Lake, and this*
> *passage reminds me of our voyage:*
>
> > *See the proud pipers on the bow,*
> > *And mark the gaudy streamers flow*
> > *From their loud chanters down, and sweep*
> > *The furrow'd bosom of the deep,*
> > *As, rushing through the lake amain,*
> > *They plied the ancient Highland strain.*

A royal salute was fired at eleven o'clock to announce the departure of the royal couple from Taymouth Castle. They drove out at the Kenmore Gate and through the dairy gate, to embark on a barge which was moored to a small jetty in the river. The royal barge, which was 32ft (9.6m) in length, had been built and fitted out by Mr McNicoll of Greenock. On each side of the bow there was a model in gold of the Breadalbane crest and a marquis's coronet, while the inside of the boat was painted to imitate the Breadalbane tartan. The seats were cushioned with the same tartan and those in the stern were fringed with gold. An awning, of finest spun silk, was also in the Breadalbane tartan and was decorated with festoons of roses, thistles and heather. The flotilla of three barges, led by the royal barge, glided under the Kenmore Bridge, while a band seated in a Thames wherry struck up the national anthem and the great throngs of people cheered and sang.

> *Our row of 16 miles up Loch Tay to Auchmore, a cottage of Lord Breadalbane's,*
> *near the end of the lake, was the prettiest thing imaginable. We saw the splendid*
> *scenery to such great advantage on both sides – Ben Lawers, with small waterfalls*
> *descending its sides, amid other high mountains wooded here and there; with*
> *Kenmore in the distance; the view, looking back, as the loch winds, was most*
> *beautiful. The boatmen sang two Gaelic boat-songs, very wild and singular; the*
> *language so guttural, and yet so soft. Captain McDougall, who steered, and who is*
> *the head of the McDougalls, showed us the real 'brooch of Lorn', which was taken*
> *by his ancestor from Robert Bruce in a battle.*

Loch Tay, some 15 miles in length, is dominated by Ben Lawers, a mountain of noble proportions, which rises to a height of almost 4,000ft (1,220m) and is the highest in Perthshire. It is renowned for its Alpine plants and is in the care of the National Trust. Loch Tayside has always been much more a pastoral than an arable farming area, because its altitude makes the successful growing of crops barely possible. Scattered across the hillsides are the ruins of croft houses and farmsteads, often beside secluded burns.

Captain McDougall, RN, in full Highland dress, commanded the royal barge. His clan had been largely absorbed by the Campbells, and in the fourteenth century became involved in a blood feud between the Comyns and Robert the Bruce. At this time they were the latter's most dangerous opponents and almost captured him in a battle in 1306. During the struggle one of McDougall's men seized Bruce and in making his escape he lost his plaid, which was

Triumphal arch at Milton of Kincraigie

fastened by a valuable brooch. Now renowned as the 'Brooch of Lorne', it remained in the possession of the McDougall chiefs for many centuries.

Lunch was taken at Auchmore at the west end of Loch Tay, near Killin, and after a brief stop the royal party continued their journey through Lochearnhead, Crieff and on to their next stop at Drummond Castle. Queen Victoria's feelings for the Breadalbanes are recorded in her diary, where she wrote: 'the kindness and attention to us of Lord and Lady Breadalbane (who is very delicate) were unbounded'.

The whole Taymouth episode was a pure delight for the royal couple, and Queen Victoria's letters were full of praise. One, to Lord Melbourne stated: 'This is a princely and most beautiful place and we have been entertained by Lord Breadalbane in a magnificent way . . . the sport he gave the Prince at shooting was on the largest scale'.

CHAPTER TWO

1844
Convalescence

BLAIR CASTLE,
WEDNESDAY 11 SEPTEMBER – TUESDAY 1 OCTOBER

THE QUEEN AT BLAIR
1844

Hail, to our lovely Queen! hail to our Higland Queen!
Welcome, thrice Welcome, to the home of the free;
All welcome again to the land of the heather,
A full Highland Welcome to Albert and thee.
Loud sounds the pibroch, and the heroes of Atholl,
The brave, and the steady, the tried, and the true,
Are belted and ready, lov'd Sovereign, to tend thee,
By their sweet native streams, and mountains so blue.
Saturday Post, Dundee

The young Queen's triumphant first visit to the Highlands had really whetted her appetite for more – she and Albert had been captivated by the magnificent scenery of the country and the generosity of its people. On 24 July 1844 Lord Glenlyon received a lengthy letter from his brother, Lord James Murray, in which he outlined the wishes of the royal couple:

*Prince Albert desired the Duke of Buccleuch to ask me whether I thought you would let Her Majesty have the use of Blair for about three weeks or so from the beginning of the last week in September. I said I thought you would be most happy to do so. Prince Albert is extremely anxious that after the Queen's confinement she should make a little trip for the benefit of her health and Blair was the place that occurred to them. They would wish to go perfectly quietly and without **any state,** in fact just as **any nobleman** would go down for a little shooting etc.*

*The Queen does not wish to inflict a 'visitation' upon you, and put you to, by paying **you** a **visit,** any expense and therefore if not inconvenient to you – would wish you to put Blair **altogether at her disposal** for about three weeks.*

An 1810 sketch of Blair Castle, showing its appearance at the time of the Queen's visit

Then come the following queries:

Will you let it? Or will you put it at her disposal without letting it? (this last is my own query). If you agree to let the Queen have it, how many bedrooms have you – for Her Majesty and attendants? How many of the royal servants can be put up? (The Duke asked me about water closets as it will be necessary to have one close to Her Majesty's room). What grouse shooting and what amount of deer forest can you let the Prince have? (He always comes in for luncheon and therefore his shooting must not be distant. I told the Duke I thought you let most of your grouse shooting). In short – if you can let Her Majesty have the house and forest; pray write the above (and any other) particulars fully – to the Duke of Buccleuch in London. In the meantime you must keep the matter **properly secret** – for it is necessary it should be kept so. The Duke of Buccleuch and Sir Robert Peel are the only persons who know of the project.

If you cannot make the arrangements – you have only to say so. Do not forget to have the 'rose' ready when Her Majesty arrives. Do not forget the water closet. I said that the Royal Party must not expect anything very **magnificent,** but that you have tolerably **comfortable** accommodation and I believe they are very easily satisfied on that head. Do not let anybody but Anne into the secret as the necessity of secrecy was strongly pointed out to me. Don't leave this letter **lying about.**

Lord Glenlyon was in Edinburgh when he received this letter and promptly wrote to Lady Glenlyon in Blair Castle, marking the letter, 'most private'. The letter starts:

My Dearest Pet,

I must entreat you as soon as you have read this, either to burn it or lock it up as it must not be known, and breathe not a syllable of its contents to a mortal being. What a god-send this will be to us if they do come. I shall write off instantly to the Duke to say that I am most happy to place Blair at Her Majesty's disposal.

Replying to the Duke of Buccleuch that day, Lord Glenlyon wrote:

I have the very greatest pleasure and heartfelt satisfaction in placing the Castle of Blair and the Forest of it entirely at Her Majesty's disposal for any length of period she may do me the honour to make use of it. I will undertake to make it as comfortable as I can in the time and I will be most proud to manage the Forest for the Prince and I think, as you know, I may venture to promise him sport provided always that the wind fits.

On 3 August Prince Albert replied:

I must write to you personally a few lines in order to express to you how much the Queen and myself feel your kindness in offering us Blair Atholl for our occupation in September. We are looking forward with the greatest pleasure to our stay in the heart of the Highlands.

Two days later the Duke of Buccleuch, Lord Privy Seal, wrote to Lord Glenlyon inform-ing him that:

The Queen and Prince Albert have expressed their great satisfaction at the Communica-tion from you respecting Blair and look forward with pleasure at the prospect of going there. I am to convey to you to impress you with the conviction that they do not want in the least any additional refinements or splendour.

The party will consist probably of the Queen, Prince Albert, Princess Royal, two ladies, two first, two second gentleman with servants.

The forest with the grouse shooting you have reserved will afford ample sport and as you have reserved the top of Glen Tilt the drives from Glen Crinie [Craoinidh] ought to be splendid and successful.

Because it was felt to be an honour and a privilege there was no question of charging the Queen for the stay in Blair Castle, and two important points kept recurring in the correspon-dence: firstly, the need for total secrecy, and secondly, the informality of the visit. It was emphasised that there was to be no repeat of the splendours of 1842. Lord James Murray met Prince Albert on 7 August and wrote next day about his 'long audience to talk over his pro-posed trip'. Prince Albert said that Queen Victoria's health was improving and he hoped to travel north around 7 September, much earlier than anticipated. He enquired about facilities for stabling, shooting and church services and whether the minister at Blair Atholl was 'all right', or from the Free Church. Lord James satisfied him on all these points, and said that there would be an adequate supply of ponies and keepers for his shooting expeditions. Albert was most anxious that 'the whole thing should be kept secret for some time longer, as the reporters get the start of him and plague him considerably and that even should the matter not be known till the last moment, there would be quite sufficient newspaper reporters at his tail'. Lord James indicated to him that the Tilt, Garry and Banvie glens would hold 'pretty near the whole of the reporters of England' and that Lord Glenlyon 'was not accustomed to stand any nonsense in Glen Tilt'.

Writing on 22 August, Lord James told his brother that Prince Albert was quite content to leave all the arrangements for shooting – keepers, dogs, powder and shot – to him and he was asked to provide housekeepers, housemaids, laundrymaids, dairymaids and one kitchen-maid. Lord Glenlyon also agreed to supply meat, poultry, dairy produce, fruit, vegetables, flour, ale, beer and porter, together with coal and forage for the horses. The royal household provided linen and plate and a baker for preparing 'plain bread'.

Provisions supplied by the Castle Home Farm amounted to £22 14s 2d.

		£
Beef	31 stones @ 5/10	9- 0-10
Mutton	26 stones @ 5/10	7-11- 8
Butter		5- 4
Milk & Cream		3- 0
Garden Vegetables		2-17- 8
Fruit		1- 3- 0
Venison	7 stones @ 4/8	1-12- 8
		£22-14- 2

Supplies from the market totalled £18 13s 8d.

		£
Bread		7-18- 4
Porter	16 gallons	1- 1- 4
Table Beer	3 Hogsheads	4-14- 0
Groceries		1-10- 0
Sundries		2- 0- 0
Oil		1-10- 0
		£18-13- 8

Wines and spirits were obtained from a local supplier, with whom an initial order for £13 6s was placed.

		£
Sherry	14 bottles @ 3/6 each	2- 9- 0
Port	8 bottles @ 3/10 each	1-10- 8
Whisky	16 bottles @ 1/4 each	1- 1- 4
Used on the 11th September		8- 5- 0
		£13- 6- 0

In spite of the implied 'informal' nature of the visit, there were over sixty servants from the royal household, falling into three categories:

UPPER SERVANTS

2 pages; 2 clerks of the kitchen; 1 cellar man; 3 cooks; 4 maids for the Queen; 1 table decker; 2 valets; 2 ladies' maids; 2 jägers (huntsmen); 1 governess; 1 nursery maid ('misery' maid); 1 hairdresser; 1 pastry cook; 1 confectioner; 1 roasting cook.

LOWER SERVANTS

1 steward's room man; 2 under butlers; 1 silver pantry man; 11 footmen; 2 messengers; 1 piper; 1 baker; 1 upholsterer.

STABLE DEPARTMENT

1 clerk of the stables; 13 stable men.

Stablemen were housed in the stable bothy, while footmen were accommodated in Old Blair and the rest stayed in the castle.

Travelling Arrangements

Ten carriages were required to transport the royal party to Blair Castle from Dundee, and for touring round during their stay: one post-chaise, a four-wheeled carriage capable of taking two or four passengers, usually with a postillion (for the Queen's use); two landaus with folding tops; one barouche, a double-seated four-wheeled carriage with folding top for ladies and equerries; two carriages for dressers, pages and maids and for the Queen's and her ladies' luggage; one columbus, a servants' brake van; one four wagon (fourgon), for baggage; and two pony carriages, sometimes called phaetons.

The Royal Household provided ten ponies and six hacks, while Lord Glenlyon was asked to supply ten Highland ponies. Queen Victoria stressed that Lord Glenlyon would 'of course only act as her *caterer* and she of course pays the bills you contract in her service for all these matters'.

Arrangements for transporting everything to the Highlands were under the control of the Earl of Jersey, Master of the Horse and on 2 September he wrote to Lord Glenlyon to tell him of his plans:

On Wednesday 4th will embark by the steamer – 8 ponies, 6 saddle horses – 2 pony phaetons: The travelling post-chaise of Her Majesty and a landau – and a Barouche. The Pony Phaetons and Horses will proceed from Dundee to Blair Atholl – I have no idea of their starting from Dundee on the day of their landing (Friday) but conceive that they will reach Dunkeld on Saturday – (resting there of course on Sunday). The two pony Phaetons will be convey'd by the ponies: so that no post-horses will be required at that time – Her Majesty's post-chaise & the Landau & Barouche, which will arrive by the steamer of 4th will await Her Majesty's arrival at Dundee –

In the whole time there will be seven carriages requiring 4 horses and a fourgon requiring a pair. It will be necessary also that a van should be hired at Dundee to convey extra luggage – Her Majesty will sail on Monday 9th at 9 o'clock from Woolwich, will land early on Wednesday at Dundee & proceed immediately on her journey.

P.S. I beg to mention that the Clerk of the Stables will require a decent bed and sitting room, at the Atholl Arms I presume, if no preparation has already been made for him in the House.

About forty horses were required for the journey from Dundee to Blair Atholl and proprietors of inns in Coupar Angus and Dunkeld were contacted and asked to provide adequate stabling and fresh horses.

It was not until 22 August, less than three weeks before the royal visit, that the *Perthshire Courier* reported the rumour that 'the Prince Consort would be visiting Blair Castle in early September to enjoy the sport of the season'. Another week passed before the *Sun* newspaper followed with a more detailed though still inaccurate account which said that 'The Royal party will visit Blair Athol, Dunkeld and Taymouth. Her Majesty will be absent about three weeks'. Next day the *Morning Post* appeared with the same story, and added that 'the sole purpose of the visit was to afford His Royal Highness an opportunity of enjoying grouse shooting and deer stalking . . .'.

The *Perthshire Advertiser* of 5 September gave prominence to the royal visit in an article on its front page entitled:

Visit of Queen and Prince Albert to Scotland
Her Majesty's loyal subjects in this (favoured) portion of her domain have been thrown into a state of anxious and pleasurable excitement by an announcement to the effect that it is the purpose of the Queen and Prince Albert again to visit the Perth-shire Highlands about the middle of next week. For some time past rumour has ascribed such an inten-tion to the Prince, with a particular view to the enjoyment of the attractive sport that is found on our Highland Hills.

Mr George Condie, the Duke's Perth agent, wrote enthusiastically of the 'prospect of Royalty once again treading the heather in Glen Tilt and seeing the antlered monarch of the forest brought down the side of Ben-y-Gloe'. George Anson, Treasurer to Prince Albert, wrote to Lord Glenlyon commending him for keeping the 'Blair secret' and commenting that it was only just appearing in the papers, while Lord James reported that he had heard it 'openly men-tioned by a Palace official on 29th August'.

So it was that, five weeks after the birth of their fourth child, Prince Alfred, the royal couple set sail in the new yacht *Victoria and Albert* from Woolwich and arrived in Dundee early on the morning of Wednesday 11 September. Their first-born, Princess Victoria, nicknamed Vicky, and then four years old, accompanied them. Later, at the age of seventeen, she was to marry Prince Frederick William, afterwards King Frederick III of Prussia. Their eldest son, William, was born in 1859 and became the Kaiser on the death of his father.

Escorting Queen Victoria on this tour were Lord Liverpool; Lord Aberdeen; Sir Robert Peel; Lord Charles Wellesley, Equerry to The Queen; Sir Edward Bowater, Equerry to the Prince; Lady Charlotte Canning, Lady in Waiting; Lady Caroline Cocks, Maid of Honour; George Anson; and Sir James Clark, the Royal Physician.

Queen Victoria's diary continues the narrative as the royal party approached Perthshire:

> *Blair Athole, Wednesday, September 11*
> *. . . Cupar Angus is a small place – a village – 14 miles from Dundee. There you enter Perthshire. We crossed the River Isla, which made me think of my poor little dog 'Isla.' For about five or six miles we went along a very pretty but rough cross-road, with the Grampians in the distance. We saw Birnam Wood and Sir W. Stewart's place in that fine valley on the opposite side of the river. All along such splendid scenery, and Albert enjoyed it so much – rejoicing in the beauties of nature, the sight of mountains, and the pure air.*

Horses were changed at Coupar Angus and the royal cavalcade crossed over the River Isla and turned off left to pass through Meikleour, close to Perthshire's famous Beech Hedge. Described by Thomas Hunter in the last century as 'one of the arboreal wonders of the world', it is 580yd (531m) long, and a hundred years ago the trees were a uniform height of 80ft (24m). It is believed to have been planted in 1746. Dunkeld is fourteen miles from Coupar Angus and the Queen arrived there at 12.30pm, approaching the town from the east along the north bank of the River Tay. Many of the roadside cottages had been cleaned, whitewashed and decorated with heather and dahlias; doorways were hung with heather, green foliage and pine branches.

In deference to the Queen's wishes, there were no triumphal arches this time and no public demonstrations of support. In Dunkeld, however, crowns and the initials 'V' and 'A' were made of daisies and fixed to several of the main buildings, while shops in Bridge Street and Atholl Street were decorated with tartans, pine branches and stag horns. A lookout was posted on the top of Newtyle Hill, just outside the town, with a commanding view of the Coupar Angus road, to give advance warning of the royal arrival.

> *The peeps of Dunkeld, with the River Tay deep in the bottom, and the view of the bridge and cathedral, surrounded by the high wooded hills, as you approached it, were lovely in the extreme. We got out at an inn (which was small but very clean) at Dunkeld, and stopped to let Vicky have some broth. Such a charming view from the window! Vicky stood and bowed to the people out of the window. There never was such a good traveler as she is, sleeping in the carriage at her usual times, not put out, not frightened at noise or crowds, but pleased and amused. She never heard the anchor go at night on board ship, but slept as sound as a top.*

A nineteenth century view of Dunkeld from the east

The carriages drew up outside the Duke of Atholl's Arms, now the Atholl Arms Hotel, built in 1833, where David Grant was the innkeeper. Here Queen Victoria, dressed in mourning with 'not a thread of colour visible save for a sprig of jasmine' and Prince Albert alighted on to a carpet of Murray tartan and spent thirty minutes eating lunch in the parlour. This time there was no 'royal luncheon' and the Princess Royal, who seems to have been an excellent traveller, was fortified with a bowl of 'weak, wholesome broth'. According to Lady Canning, she sat waiting patiently, 'looking at 2 basins of strong giblet soup and Athole Brose and short-bread and other unwholesome good things'. The crowd in the street cheered rapturously when Princess Victoria appeared at the window and bowed to them several times.

Shortly after leaving Dunkeld, which is 20 miles from Blair, and 15 from Cupar Angus, we met Lord Glenlyon in a carriage; he jumped out, and rode with us the whole way to Blair – and a most beautiful road it is. Six miles on, in the woods to the left, we could see Kinnaird House, where the late Lady Glenlyon (Lord Glenlyon's mother, who died about two or three months ago) used to live.

Dunkeld in the mid-nineteenth century. The Duke of Atholl's Arms is on the right

The Road to Blair

On the departure from Dunkeld a battery on Stanley Hill fired a farewell salute to the royal couple and at the outskirts of the town the royal party was joined by Lord Glenlyon. This time the Queen's route was along the east bank of the Tay, following the road which only in recent years has been replaced by the new A9. This was the road to Atholl:

> There are some that love the Borderland and
> some the Lothians wide,
> And some would boast the Neuk o' Fife and
> some the banks o' Clyde;
> And some are fair for Mull and Skye and
> all the Western Sea,
> But the road that runs by Atholl will
> be doing yet fine for me.

Kinnaird House was bought in 1830 by the 4th Duke and, following Lord Glenlyon's marriage in 1839 his mother, the Dowager Lady Glenlyon moved in and made considerable alterations. She was born in 1789 as Lady Emily Percy, second daughter of the 2nd Duke of Northumberland, thus uniting two great families, from the north-east of England and the Central Highlands. Lady Emily died, after an illness lasting several months, on 21 June 1844, less than three months before the Queen's visit. She was buried in Dunkeld Cathedral, and Kinnaird House was then let out as a shooting lodge.

> *Then we passed the point of Logierait, where there are the remains of an ancient castle – the old Regality Court of the Dukes of Athole. At Moulinearn we tasted some of the 'Athole brose', which was brought to the carriage.*

Logierait is situated near the confluence of the rivers Tay and Tummel and for centuries was the seat of the Regality Court of the Lords of Atholl, who wielded absolute power in the district. In those days the village had its own jail, gallows and courthouse, said to be the 'noblest house in Perthshire', with a 70ft (21m) courtroom and galleries at each end. Logierait means 'hollow of the castle', and the remains of an old castle were visible in the last century to the north of the village. At that time a remarkable ash tree, reputed to be over a thousand years old, still stood in the garden of the Logierait Hotel. This was the scene of the last public hanging in the district, when a local man was executed. Apparently the rope broke three times, but the onlookers' pleas for mercy were to no avail.

The next stop was at the old inn at Moulinearn, where the horses were changed and Atholl brose was brought to the carriage. By then Moulinearn was a telegraph station, part of a communication network in the Highlands. When the Dunkeld battery signalled the Queen's departure this was heard here and a Union Jack was immediately run up a flagpole. This was spotted from the top of Craigower, a dominant hill north of Pitlochry, where another flag was raised. The summit of Craigower is clearly visible from Blair Castle, so that within ten minutes of her leaving Dunkeld those at Blair were aware of the Queen's progress. As she left Moulinearn, a second Union Jack was raised and answered on Craigower.

> *We passed Pitlochrie, a small village, Faskally, a very pretty place of Mr Butter's to the left, and then came to the Pass of Killiecrankie, which is quite magnificent; the road winds along it, and you look down a great height, all wooded on both sides, the Garry rolling below it. I cannot describe how beautiful it is. Albert was in perfect ecstasies.*

Pitlochry lies three miles north of Moulinearn and here many of the houses were decked out with flowers, heather, greenery and several Union Jacks. Originally the town consisted of three small hamlets, with an inn and a small distillery in the western village. A school was situated in the eastern hamlet and a meal mill, fed by the Moulin Burn, was in the middle. As the royal entourage left Pitlochry, huge bonfires were lit on the tops of two of the hills overlooking the town, Craigower and Dunfallandy Hill. Faskally, formerly Dysart, for centuries owned by a cadet house of the Robertsons but by 1844 owned by Mr Archibald Butter, a Lieutenant in the Atholl Highlanders, was a large estate of over 17,500 acres with fine policy woodlands – some of the trees are now over 200 years old.

The Farragon range, described as very Swiss-looking by Prince Albert in 1842, seen here from the top of Castle Dow

General Wade's magnificent bridge spanning the Tay at Aberfeldy

Castle Menzies, the medieval stronghold of one of the clans which greeted the Queen at Taymouth Castle in 1842

'There were a number of Lord Breadalbane's Highlanders, all in the Campbell tartan, drawn up in front of the house . . .' – Queen Victoria (1842)

The secret door in the library, disguised as a bookcase at Taymouth Castle

The Kenmore Gate, west entrance to Taymouth Castle

The royal couple pausing to admire the view in the Pass of Killiecrankie

Killiecrankie

Queen Victoria paused at the summit of the Pass of Killiecrankie to admire the wooded scenery and the River Garry below. Here she spoke to William MacDonald, a local resident, who from this vantage point explained the Battle of Killiecrankie, which had taken place on 27 July 1689. He told the Queen about the battle fought between 3,000 Government troops with their well-armed cavalry under General McKay, and 2,500 Highlanders with only a few horses, commanded by Viscount Claverhouse ('Bonnie Dundee'). The Protestant rulers, William and Mary had ascended to the throne the year before, but Scotland's loyalty was divided. The Stuart dynasty had ruled Scotland for 300 years and loyalties, especially in the Highlands, ran deep. The Jacobite supporters of James VII of Scotland found a leader in Bonnie Dundee, who set about raising a Highland army, and on 27 July he stationed his men on a ridge on high ground, overlooking the north end of the pass. Down below, government troops emerging from the pass halted on level ground and for two hours the armies faced each other and waited. About seven o'clock in the evening Dundee gave the order to charge and, before the regular troops could fix their bayonets after the first volley, the Highlanders were on them, wielding their broadswords with devastating and bloody effect. In less than an hour the government troops were put to flight. Dundee, however, was killed and his body was brought to Blair and laid in the vault of St Bride's Church.

'The house is a large plain white building' – Queen Victoria

Lude, Mr McInroy's, to the right, is very pretty. Blair Athole is only four or five miles from the Killiecrankie Pass. Lord Glenlyon has had a new approach made. The house is a large plain white building, surrounding by high hills, which one can see from the windows. Lord and Lady Glenlyon, with their little boy, received us at the door, and showed us to our rooms, and then left us.

Lude, created a barony in 1448, was for centuries a stronghold of the Robertsons. Lude House, with commanding views across Glen Garry, was built on the site of an earlier house in the mid-1820s. The estate was purchased by the McInroy family in 1821, and at that time was described as:

> . . . *a beautiful estate . . . resting on a bed of primitive limestone and marble, rendering the pasture superior in quality to most in the Highlands, while the arable land, being of a rich loam, is capable of returning the weightiest and best produce of grain of all sorts, as well as of green crops. The low grounds are, for the most part, inclosed and subdivided by substantial stone fences and the estate is intersected with good roads affording every facility of Communication.*

The royal cavalcade crossed over the Tilt Bridge, built twenty years earlier by the Commission for Roads and Bridges when they were re-routing and upgrading the old military road. They arrived at the main entrance to Blair Castle at three o'clock, where a detachment of

Atholl Highlanders formed the guard of honour and took over from the Scots Greys who had escorted the Queen from Dundee. The Atholl Highlanders were commanded by Captain Oswald of Dunnikier (a second cousin to Lord Glenlyon) who died in 1893 after completing more than fifty years' service with the regiment. It had already been agreed that the Atholl Highlanders would provide the security guard for the royal couple, and Queen Victoria 'with great pleasure' accepted their services. A police inspector, who knew 'most of the regular royal tormentors' was also in attendance, accompanied by two constables. A couple of plain-clothes officers were provided to mingle with the crowd in case the Queen was 'troubled by idle people anxious to stare'. They were described by the *Perthshire Advertiser* as 'idling about with their hands in their pockets and enjoying a most uninterrupted sinecure'.

Blair Castle

As the cavalcade passed through the entrance, the Atholl Highlanders formed up on each side and escorted the royal couple up the main avenue to the castle. The avenue, formerly a grass track called Gregor's Walk, was turned into a gravelled drive in time for the Queen's visit and the avenue of lime trees was extended to form the main approach to the castle.

Blair Castle, at the heart of the land of Atholl and its history, spans more than 700 years. Tradition states that when Henry Stewart, the last Celtic Earl of Atholl, was away fighting in the Crusades, John the Red Comyn invaded Atholl and built Comyn's Tower, four storeys high, in 1269, which is still incorporated in the north-west part of the main castle building. Very little is known about the castle for the next 250 years. It was enlarged in the sixteenth century with a square, battlemented tower of seven storeys, a new round tower and two storeys added to Comyn's Tower. At this period it was little more than a large hunting lodge, as the main residence of the family was at Dunkeld. John Stewart, 3rd Earl of Atholl from 1521 to 1542, was famous for his hospitality and built a two-storey extension, which included a large banqueting hall. In the seventeenth century the castle was described as being 'irregular and very high with walls of great thickness, having Comyn's Tower projecting from the west end of the front of the house'. This was at the time of the Montrose campaign in 1644, when the castle was garrisoned by Cromwellian troops and became unfit for habitation.

In 1736 James, 2nd Duke, employed an architect called Mr Douglas to modify the castle, and he completed the unfinished part on the south-west end by adding another floor and building on two more rooms. Seven years later another architect, Mr Winter, was employed and work started on a detached two-storey building known as the south wing, but the 1745 Jacobite uprising put a temporary halt to this. William, the Jacobite Duke and eldest surviving son of the 1st Duke, took possession of Blair Castle, and Charles Edward Stuart stayed here for three days during his triumphant march to England in 1745. Within two days of the Jacobite troops departing, Cumberland's forces gained control and were then besieged for three weeks by Lord George Murray, but his siege guns were ineffective and little damage was done.

Immediately after the '45, the 2nd Duke set about rebuilding, but he was determined to ensure that the castle was never again garrisoned and that henceforth it would cease to be a

BLAIR CASTLE, 1736
FRONT ELEVATION

Blair Castle from the east in 1736

fortress. Thus plans were drawn up to 'clip' the castle and upon completion it resembled a large, square-plan Georgian mansion house. Building work took ten years and the castle was reduced in height, with two storeys being removed from Comyn's Tower and the battlements, pepper box turrets and crow-step gables taken down. Although Duke James radically altered and perhaps disfigured the exterior, the interior was greatly improved by re-dividing the rooms and decorating throughout with excellent taste. The banqueting hall was transformed into a magnificent dining room with the grandeur of a heavily modelled stucco ceiling, marble chimneypiece and exquisite furniture. The drawing room, which until a few weeks before the Queen's arrival had been used as a timber store, was transformed in great haste, walls decorated in crimson damask to show off the white marble chimneypieces designed by Thomas Carter. It was furnished with eighteenth-century gilt chairs and settees to make a grand setting for the Queen's visit.

A crowd of nearly a thousand people gathered in the grounds as the royal couple crossed the Banvie to reach the lawn in front of the castle, where four pipers were playing *The Prince's Salute* and two three-pounder guns fired a royal salute. Captain John Drummond of the Atholl Highlanders had located the artillery pieces in the Woolwich Arsenal and arranged for their transport to Blair especially for this royal occasion. Four gunners were posted to each gun and training was provided by artillery men from Leith Fort.

Victoria and Albert were received at the front door of the castle by Lord and Lady Glenlyon and their son John George, Marquis of Tullibardine (the title given to the heir to the

Lady Glenlyon at Blair Castle

dukedom). He was born in 1840 and was therefore the same age as the Princess Royal. He succeeded his father in 1864, to become the 7th Duke.

There has been some confusion in the past as to where the royal couple slept in the castle, but a rough sketch by the Queen in the Windsor archives showing the 'View from the window of Albert's dressing room at Blair Athole Sept: 29 – 1844', has revealed the exact location. The sketch shows a tower with a single battlement and flat roof exactly opposite the window, with several hills in the distance. The tower is the Clock Tower, which until 1900 had a flat roof, so that Albert's dressing room has been identified as what is now the Derby Dressing Room. Queen Victoria's bedroom was the Derby Room next door, and her own dressing room was the Red Bedroom adjacent to the Drawing Room. This concurs with Lady Canning's description, as she recorded that 'On the 2nd floor the Queen is lodged at the top of the house'. The Queen's sitting room, into which a piano was hurriedly installed, was nearby and two rooms were set aside for the Princess Royal, one as a bedroom for herself and her nurse, the other being a small sitting room. Two of the Queen's maids were in another room and a third maid slept in her dressing room.

A bouquet of freshly-pulled heather and a pitcher of water from the Queen's Well in Glen Tilt were placed in the Queen's bedroom every day. The Queen's Well is about four miles from the castle, opposite the confluence of Allt Mhairc and the River Tilt, where beside the glen road there is a fine spring of pure, clear water issuing from the hillside.

Atholl Highlanders

Within a few minutes of his arrival Prince Albert, accompanied by Lord Aberdeen, Lord Liverpool, Lord Wellesley and Lord Glenlyon, inspected the Atholl Highlanders, drawn up in line in front of the castle. The regiment consisted of ten officers, five sergeants, four pipers and 140 rank and file, divided into four companies:

'A' Company: *Captain John Drummond of Megginch*; minimum height without shoes 6ft; arms: Lochaber axes.

'B' Company: *Captain James Oswald of Dunnikier*; minimum height without shoes 5ft 10½in; arms: muskets and bayonets.

'C' Company: *Captain Charles Home-Drummond of Blair Drummond*; minimum height without shoes 5ft 9¼in; arms: broadswords and targets.

'D' Company: *Captain James Alston-Stewart of Urrard*; minimum height without shoes 5ft 8in; arms: broadswords and targets.

After inspection the Atholl Highlanders paraded in front of Prince Albert, led by four pipers playing a pibroch. A marquee in striped silk with two 6ft (1.8m) wall tents and a small officers' marquee were pitched in front of the castle to house the guard. This was composed of a captain, two lieutenants, two sergeants, one piper and twenty rank and file. Six sentries were permanently posted throughout the Queen's stay.

The Highlanders took their guard duty seriously and were authorised to arrest anyone without a pass. One of these unfortunates was Willie Duff, a 6ft 3in tall Highlander with a luxuriant beard which earned him the nickname 'Beardy WIllie'. He had entered the service of the Atholl family in 1839 and made violins and cellos in his spare time. He was described as a 'savage, picturesque keeper with a long black beard', who was kept prisoner in the tent all night because for the third time he had attempted to pass the sentry without a pass. As punishment he was given bread and water for breakfast and was not permitted to carry the standard at the next parade. Another instance was when Lord James Murray, who arrived late, was refused entry as he did not have the necessary countersigned pass, although he offered to write his own!

The Atholl Highlanders were formed in 1777, when the 4th Duke offered to raise a thousand men to serve for three years in America during the War of Independence. The regiment never embarked for America and instead was posted to Ireland, returning in 1782. Next year they were ordered to India and marched to Portsmouth for embarkation but, fearing a mutiny as the three-year enlistment had long since ended, the regiment was disbanded. During her stay at the castle the Queen announced her intention of presenting two colours to the regiment in recognition of their services in 1842 and 1844. These were presented on 4 September 1845 in the presence of Prince George of Cambridge and Prince Edward of Saxe-Weimar by Lady Glenlyon on behalf of the Queen. Today the Atholl Highlanders are Europe's only remaining private army, and have the right to bear arms.

On the night of the Queen's arrival huge bonfires blazed on several of the prominent hills round the castle, such as Carn Liath and Tulach.

The striped silk marquee and tents to house the guard, by Charles Landseer (R L 19542)

> *Blair Castle, Blair Athole,*
> *Thursday, September 12.*
>
> *We took a delightful walk of two hours. Immediately near the house the scenery is very wild, which is most enjoyable. The moment you step out of the house you see those splendid hills all round. We went to the left through some neglected pleasure-grounds, and then through the wood, along a steep winding path overhanging the rapid stream. These Scotch streams, full of stones, and clear as glass, are most beautiful: the peeps between the trees, the depth of the shadows, the mossy stones mixed with slate etc which cover the banks, are lovely; at every turn you have a picture. We were up high, but could not get to the top; Albert in such delight; it is a happiness to see him, he is in such spirits.*

Queen Victoria's routine during her stay was strictly adhered to. She rose at seven o'clock following the sound of a pibroch played under her window by her personal piper,

Angus MacKay and breakfast was served between eight and nine o'clock, following a short walk in the grounds, which lie in an open situation and are defined by a series of avenues, footpaths and rows of trees that radiate out towards the perimeter from the castle and garden. The Princess Royal was taken out every morning for walking and riding on a Shetland pony and was described as a 'quick, lively and entertaining girl'. Being the same age as Lord Glenlyon's son John, they often played together and were sometimes seen walking arm in arm. Lunch was served at two o'clock, after which carriages were ready at three for a drive. Dinner was timed for eight o'clock.

Thursday was a beautiful day and Queen Victoria and Prince Albert walked for two hours in the grounds, with a wheelchair kept at the ready in case she tired. They walked to Diana's Grove, named after Diana, goddess of hunting, which was laid out as a flower garden in 1737 and later planted with exotic trees. A statue of Diana with a deer stands at the central point, from which a number of paths radiate outwards. One of these led to a circular summer house called the Temple of Fame, erected in 1751. In it was an inner ring of plaster busts of philosophers like Plato, writers such as Shakespeare and scientists like Newton, with an outer ring which depicted the four seasons. It fell down in 1864 and was not rebuilt. By the time of the Queen's visit Diana's Grove had become a wilderness and it was not until the 1870s that it was cleared and replanted. This two acre site contains an immense variety of specimen trees and it is unlikely that there is anywhere else containing such a diverse range of ages and species in such a small area.

Old Blair

We came back by a higher drive, then went to the Factor's house, still higher up, where Lord and Lady Glenlyon are living, having given Blair up to us. We walked out to a corn-field where a number of women were cutting and reaping the oats ('shearing' as they call it in Scotland), with a splendid view of the hills before us, so rural and romantic, so unlike our daily Windsor walk (delightful as that is); and this change does such good – as Albert observes, it refreshes one for a long time. We then went into the kitchen-garden, and to a walk from which there is a magnificent view. This mixture of great wilderness and art is perfection.

The Queen and Albert walked beside the Banvie Burn to Old Blair, where they saw St Bride's, the old parish church which is mentioned in the Bagimond Roll of 1275, when it paid a tithe of four merks to Rome. Some of the church may be Celtic, but most of it dates from the sixteenth century. It was surveyed in 1820, and although the roof had completely gone the walls were sound, and it was rebuilt. However, within three years a decision was taken to build a new church on the Haugh of Blair beside the new road, so once again St Bride's fell into disuse. In 1844 it was in a ruinous state, but some of the roof was still intact. St Bride's contains the vault where 'Bonnie Dundee' was buried, and to commemorate the bicentenary of the Battle of Killiecrankie the 7th Duke placed a stone tablet in the wall with the following inscription:

> Within the vault beneath
> are interred the remains of
> JOHN GRAHAM OF CLAVERHOUSE
> VISCOUNT DUNDEE
> who fell at the Battle of Killiecrankie
> 27 July 1689 aged 46
> This memorial is placed here by
> JOHN 7TH DUKE OF ATHOLE K.T.

The whole of Blair Castle was put at the Queen's disposal for her visit, and the Glenlyons moved out to the Factor's House in Old Blair, then the home of a Captain MacDuff. Until the re-routing of the military road in the 1820s it had been an inn called Tigh Glas, which appears in a charter of 1504 as 'Le Ale House with Croft in le kirktoun of Blare'. When the military road was built in the 1720s alterations and additions were made, the inn being enlarged to seventeen rooms, a new brew-house installed and new stables built for twenty-six horses. There seems to be some confusion about what was happening in the cornfield beside the road behind Tibby's Lodge. The Queen described a 'number of women cutting and reaping the oats', unlike the *Illustrated London News* which reported that:

> Her Majesty and Prince Albert have been to the old village of Blair to the lodge, where there was a party of shearers at work shearing sheep. Her Majesty and the Prince remained for some time looking on, highly amused with the proceedings. There were some fine Scotch terriers with the shearers, of which the Queen took great notice, patting and playing with them.

The kitchen garden is known as Hercules Garden, which was laid out in the 1740s when the 2nd Duke started planning his policy parks and grounds. It was graphically described by Bishop Pocock when he paid a visit to Blair in 1760:

In the whole length of the kitchen garden the Duke has made a fine piece of water with six or more islands and peninsulas on it, two of which are for swans to breed on, having thatched houses built on them for that purpose and the wild ducks breed on the islands. The garden is formed on a gentle declivity on both sides, all walled round.

Elsewhere he saw twenty 'grotesque' figures, a pigeon house, gardener's cottage and a glass-fronted semi-circular summerhouse at the south-east end. He described the walk leading to a huge statue of Hercules and believed it was 'the most beautiful kitchen garden in the world'.

Glen Tilt

At a little before four o'clock Albert drove me out in the pony phaeton till nearly six – such a drive! Really to be able to sit on one's pony carriage, and to see such wild, beautiful scenery as we did, the farthest point being only five miles from the house, is an immense delight. We drove along Glen Tilt, through a wood overhanging the River Tilt, which joins the Garry, and as we left the wood we came upon such a lovely view – Ben-y-Ghlo straight before us – and under these high hills the River Tilt gushing and winding over stones and slates, and the hills and mountains skirted at the bottom with beautiful trees – the whole lit up by the sun – and the air so pure and fine; but no description can at all do it justice, or give an idea of what this drive was.

Oh! what can equal the beauties of nature! What enjoyment there is in them! Albert enjoys it so much; he is in ecstasies here. He has inherited this love for nature from his dear father. We went as far as the Marble Lodge, a keeper's cottage, and came back the same way.

This day marked the start of Queen Victoria's love affair with Glen Tilt, and she returned to it again and again during her stay, sometimes walking and at other times in a carriage. She was totally captivated by its rugged grandeur and spent several hours on each of successive days in the glen. She made a reference to it in her diary on 30 September 1859, during an 'expedition' to Inchrory in Glen Avon:

As we approached Inchrory (a shooting lodge of Lord H. Bentick's), the scenery became finer and finer, reminding us of Glen Tilt, and was most beautiful at Inchrory, with the fine, broad water of the Avon flowing down from the mountains.

Glen Tilt is sixteen miles long from its confluence with the River Garry to the watershed on the Perthshire/Aberdeenshire boundary. A hundred years before the Queen's visit it was an important east–west route linking Blair Atholl with Braemar, which came to public notice in the 1850s following the 6th Duke's unsuccessful attempt to close it to travellers. At one time it had a population of about 500 people and the remains of their villages and shielings are still visible along its length. Marble Lodge was built around 1815 and named after the nearby marble quarry a few hundred yards upstream. The presence of a marble seam was first brought to the 4th Duke's notice in 1813 following a visit by the Scottish Geological Society and by the next year marble blocks were being sent to Dundee for shipment to London. The famous green Glen Tilt marble began appearing in stately homes and public buildings as plinths, chimney-pieces and in furniture, yet as early as 1844 it was no longer economic because of cheap imports and production virtually ceased.

Next day, Friday 13 September, was showery but this did not prevent Albert from having his first morning's shoot and he returned for lunch with 4½ brace of grouse and a blackcock. Elaborate plans were drawn up for the Prince's shooting expeditions and the estate keepers were split up into three parties as follows:

A guard of honour of Atholl Highlanders outside the church

1st Party: *Peter Fraser, Jock McAra, Donald Gow, Sandy Robertson, Sandy McAra, James Fraser and Donald Stewart* with two horses;
2nd Party: *John McPherson, Charlie Fraser, John Stewart and Willie Duff* with one horse;
3rd Party: *Jock Robertson* with two men and a horse.

That evening the two Officers of the Watch were invited to dine in the castle. One was Captain John Drummond of Megginch and the other was the Hon William Drummond, the Master of Strathallan, who wore the sword used by his great grandfather when he was killed at the Battle of Culloden nearly a hundred years earlier. The Master of Strathallan owned a 'Calotype machine', a very early camera, which he set up one day just above the guard tents in front of the castle. Lady Canning recorded that in one of his pictures 'Car (Lady Caroline Cocks) & I with the same gun for a background succeeded very well, all but our faces, for we made grimaces in the sun & laughed besides, when the spectators peeped at us'.

The Queen indicated that regardless of the weather she would go to church at Blair the next Sunday and insisted that Lady Glenlyon sat next to her in the pew to help her follow the service, to which she was not accustomed. George Anson informed the minister, Mr Irvine, that the service should not be longer than 1½ hours and that the Queen was in the habit of listening to a sermon which lasted about 25 minutes. On Sunday 15 September, therefore, the

Queen and Prince Albert, accompanied by Lady Canning and Lady Cocks and escorted by the Atholl Highlanders, attended church on the Haugh of Blair. The royal pew, slightly raised and opposite the pulpit, was handsomely lined with crimson satin, cushioned and carpeted. The Queen, wearing a black satinette gown and mantle with a white bonnet, listened intently to the minister, whose text for the sermon was taken from St Matthew, Chapter 5, Verse 13: *Ye are the salt of the earth*. His sermon was a 'plain, straightforward discourse, devoid of all flourishes of rhetoric'.

Falls of Bruar

Monday September 16.

After our luncheon at half past three, Albert drove me (Lord Glenlyon riding with us) to the Falls of Bruar. We got out at the road, and walked to the upper falls, and down again by the path on the opposite side. It is a walk of three miles round, and a very steep ascent; at every turn the view of the rushing falls is extremely fine, and looking back on the hills, which were so clear and so beautifully lit up with the rapid stream below, was most exquisite. We threw stones down to see the effect in the water. The trees which surround the falls were planted by the late Duke of Athole in compliance with Burns's 'Petition' ('The Humble Petition of Bruar Water to the noble Duke of Athole').

The evening was beautiful, and we feasted our eyes on the ever-changing, splendid views of the hills and vales as we drove back. Albert said that the chief beauty of the mountain scenery consisted in its frequent changes. We came home at six oclock.

Monday was fine and at their third attempt Queen Victoria and Prince Albert success-fully reached the Falls of Bruar, three miles to the west. The two earlier attempts on the Friday and Saturday were abandoned because of the weather, but the Queen was determined to see one of Perthshire's more spectacular beauty spots early in her stay. Visitors to the falls in the eighteenth century saw a bare, open hillside, awesome in its desolation until trees were first planted by Planter John in 1797. At the age of twenty-eight Robert Burns set out on his only tour of the Highlands and in August 1787 stayed in Blair Castle as the guest of the 4th Duke. He spent a short time at the falls and afterwards wrote his *Humble Petition of Bruar Water to the Duke of Athole*. In this poem Burns adopts the guise of the river and pleads with the Duke to plant the bare banks with trees. Verse five in the poem seems to capture the poet's sentiment:

> *Would, then, my noble master please*
> *To grant my highest wishes?*
> *He'll shade my banks wi' tow'ring trees,*
> *And bonie spreading bushes.*
> *Delighted doubly then, my Lord,*
> *You'll wander on my banks,*
> *And listen mony a grateful bird*
> *Return you tuneful thanks.*

Robert Burns died in 1796 with his vision of Bruar unfulfilled and it was only his death that spurred the Duke to begin planting. Within a few months 60,000 larch and an equal amount of Scots pine trees were planted and only a year after the poet's death a new wild garden was created in his memory. A number of summerhouses, grottoes and viewhouses were built beside the path where the best views of the three falls could be gained. By 1844 the trees were mature and Burns' objection to the bare hillside was removed. The farm at Bridge of Bruar was converted into an inn to accommodate the many visitors to the falls and was only closed with the coming of the railway in 1863.

Queen Victoria's visit, which came after several days of heavy rain, meant that the falls were at their spectacular best, rushing down as a raging torrent as described in Fullarton's *Imperial Gazetteer of Scotland*:

> Her Majesty was drawn up the greater part of the pathway in her garden chair as the fatigue would have been too great of ascending to such a height. Lord Glenlyon acted as guide, and pointed out the beauties of the place to the royal visitors. Her Majesty was drawn in her chair up the pathway to the first bridge, where the grotto affords a beautiful panoramic view of the waterfall, and she then proceeded across the bridge to the right side of the pass (as you go up), and ascended beyond the second grotto up to the very top of the pass, further indeed than visitors are generally taken by the ordinary guides.

Throughout the three-week stay many visitors and tourists flocked to the district, hoping to catch a glimpse of the royal couple. Both hotels were crowded out and it was reported that some were glad to be allowed to sleep under dining room tables and every bedroom had three or four inmates. Mr Macpherson, proprietor of the Blair Atholl Inn, was contracted to supply the castle guard with provisions, costs to be charged to the Queen's account. At this time it was just a small coaching inn, having opened in 1832 following the closure of Tigh Glas in Old Blair.

Tuesday, September 17.

At a quarter to four o'clock we drove out, Albert driving me, and the ladies and Lord Glenlyon following in another carriage. We drove to the Pass of Killiecrankie, which looked in its greatest beauty and splendor, and appeared quite closed, so that one could not imagine how one was to get out of it. We drove over a bridge to the right, where the view of the pass both ways, with the Garry below, is beautiful. We got out a little way beyond this and walked on a mile to the Falls of Tummel, the stream of which is famous for salmon: these falls, however, are not so fine, or nearly so high, as those of the Bruar. We got home at half past six; the day was fast fading, and the lights were lovely.

We watched two stags fighting just under our window: they are in an enclosure, and roar incessantly.

The Falls of Tummel: '. . . these falls, however, are not so fine, or nearly so high, as those of the Bruar . . .'
– Queen Victoria

The York Cascade in the last century, now a mere trickle

On Tuesday morning the Queen took her usual walk after breakfast in the company of Lady Glenlyon. They walked again through Hercules Garden and reached the Grotto overlooking the River Tilt and opposite a cascade. The Grotto was built in 1740 at a time when the castle grounds were being landscaped, and the cataract they saw was the York Cascade, named after the Archbishop of York. The cascade was formed by the spill over of the mill lade for the various watermills in Old Bridge of Tilt, as it plunged 50ft (15m) to the river below.

Robert Heron, the eighteenth-century traveller, described the scene in 1790:

I was carried by my conductor by paths, the line of which I recollect not, to a grotto in front of which poured a cataract. Within this grotto was a mossy seat – a scene where a hermit might forget the world and indulge in undisturbed meditation on the wonders of nature. Spars, varieties of quartz disposed with some ores are disposed through the rude walls: from the roof hang stalactites.

Meanwhile Prince Albert, with Lord Glenlyon and Lord Wellesley, went shooting on Struan Point and bagged 15 brace of grouse. Struan Point lies below An Teampan, the conspicuous 1,500ft (450m) hill four miles west of the castle which provides commanding panoramic views along Glen Garry. The summit is a mysterious place, ringed with an ancient stone wall and planted with larch trees in a circle. Many of the trees on the west side have gone but those to leeward, though fallen, have taken root again and substantial growth has issued from the fallen trunks.

That afternoon the royal party drove out to Killiecrankie, passing on their way the Claverhouse stone in a flat field below Urrard House, where Bonnie Dundee allegedly fell during the battle in 1689. Once again the Queen paused to talk to William MacDonald, before turning right near the foot of the pass to cross the river by the old Garry Bridge. A party of eighteen people were crossing the river in an overcrowded ferry boat near this point in 1767 when it capsized and everyone on board was drowned apart from the ferryman himself, whose wife rescued him with a boathook. Three years later the Garry Bridge, an impressive single-arched stone bridge with a large circular 'window' to relieve pressure in times of spate, was built by public subscription. It was taken down in the 1950s. The party halted at the top of the brae across the bridge, where the Queen got out and walked for a mile beside the River Garry until she reached its confluence with the Tummel. She spent forty-five minutes admiring the beauties of the Falls of Tummel, a well-known beauty spot where, through erosion, the softer layers and weaker rocks have worn away, leaving the harder layers to form the outcrops and cascades in the river bed. The falls are at their dramatic best after heavy rain or a rapid thaw. A small stone memorial was later erected below the falls to commemorate this visit.

Climbing Tulach

Wednesday, September 18

At nine o'clock we set off on ponies to go up one of the hills, Albert riding the dun pony and I the gray, attended only by Lord Glenlyon's excellent servant, Sandy

Fording the Garry: '. . . Sandy leading my pony and Albert following closely, the water reaching up above Sandy's knees' – Queen Victoria

McAra, in his Highland dress. We went out by the back way across the road, and to the left through the ford, Sandy leading my pony and Albert following closely, the water reaching up above Sandy's knees. We then went up the hill of Tulloch, first straight up a very steep cabbage-field, and then in a zigzag manner round, till we got up to the top; the ponies scrambling up over stones and every thing, and never making a false step; and the view all round being splendid and most beautifully lit up. We went to the very highest top, which can not be seen from the house or from below; and from here the view is like a panorama: you see the Falls of Bruar, Ben-y-Chat, Ben Vrackie, Ben-y-Ghlo, the Killiecrankie Pass, and a whole range of distant hills on the other side, which one can not at all see from below. In the direction of Taymouth you also see Dalnacardoch, the first stage from Blair. Blair itself and the houses in the village looked like little toys from the great height we were on. It was quite romantic. Here we were, with only this Highlander behind us holding the ponies (for we got off twice and walked about) – not a house, not a creature near us, but the pretty Highland sheep, with their horns and black faces – up at the top of Tulloch, surrounded by beautiful mountains.

We came back the same way that we went, and stopped at the ford to let the ponies drink before we rode through. We walked from inside the gate, and came home at half past eleven – the most delightful, most romantic ride and walk I ever

Rock Lodge, home of Mrs Macnaughton in 1842

An 1815 map of Blair Castle showing the layout of the parks and gardens. From 1749 to 1831 it was called
Atholl House, after which it was renamed Blair Castle

The Banner Hall, setting for the grand ball in Taymouth Castle

The Dowager Lady Glenlyon

The drawing room, in use as a lumber room prior to the royal visit

'We went to the left through some neglected pleasure grounds' – Queen Victoria. Diana's Grove with its statue of the goddess

'. . . and from here the view is like a panorama . . .' – Queen Victoria. A nineteenth century view from near the summit of Tulach

had. I had never been up such a mountain, and then the day was so fine. The hill of Tulloch is covered with grass, and is so delightfully soft to walk upon.

Queen Victoria, dressed in black with a shepherd's tartan shawl and riding a grey High-land pony and Albert, clad in plaid trousers, shooting jacket and a white hat, riding a dun pony, left the castle at nine o'clock escorted solely by Sandy McAra, an Atholl hillman. They rode down the castle back drive, passed the Atholl Arms Hotel, and turned right down Ford Road by the corn mill, which has been in existence since the early seventeenth century and was initially a single storey building thatched with straw and turf. It was altered in 1747 and again completely rebuilt and enlarged around the time of the Queen's visit. At that time there was a second mill, a lint mill, across the mill lade but this has long since disappeared.

Sandy McAra led the royal pair through the Garry ford at the foot of the road and then through a field of turnips (rather than cabbages!) to climb to the top of Tulach Hill, which at 1,500ft (458m) dominates Blair Atholl from the south. Here, as the Queen herself described, the scene is breathtaking, with all the hills of Atholl appearing in a vast panoramic amphi-theatre. With only a stalwart Highlander as guide and escort, someone, according to the *Perth-shire Advertiser* was heard to say: 'She kens brawly she's in the Hielands – naebody'll hurt her here.' Lady Canning recorded that Sandy McAra was very proud of being the Queen's guide and no one could persuade him to talk about it. 'It's no for me to tell all that Her Majesty talked about,' he said. Later that afternoon the Prince shot a half-tame stag from the dining room window, and it seems that no one enjoyed the scene. The Princess Royal wept bitterly, and whilst it made the Queen shake, she could not resist watching again when the performance was repeated the next day.

> *Thursday, September 19*
>
> *Albert set off, immediately after luncheon, deer-stalking, and I was to follow and wait below in order to see the deer driven down. At four o'clock I set off with Lady Glenlyon and Lady Canning, Mr Oswald and Lord Charles Wellesley riding, by the lower Glen Tilt drive. We stopped at the end, but were still in the wood; Sandy was looking out and watching. After waiting we were allowed to come out of the carriage, and came upon the road, where we saw some deer on the brow of the hill. We sat down on the ground, Lady Canning and I sketching, and Sandy and Mr Oswald, both in Highland costume (the same that they all wear here, viz., a gray cloth jacket and waistcoat, with a kilt and a Highland bonnet), lying on the grass and looking through glasses. After waiting again some time, we were told in a mysterious whisper that 'they were coming,' and indeed a great herd did appear on the brow of the hill, and came running down a good way, when, most provokingly, two men who were walking on the road – which they had no business to have done – suddenly came in sight, and then the herd all ran back again, and the sport was spoiled. After waiting some little while we observed Albert, Lord Glenlyon, and the keepers on the brow of the hill, and then we got into the carriage, drove a little way, went over the bridge, where there is a shepherd's 'shiel', and got out and waited for them to join us, which they did almost immediately, looking very picturesque with their rifles. My poor Albert had not even fired one shot for fear of spoiling the whole thing but had been running about a good deal. The group of keepers and dogs was very pretty. After talking and waiting a little while, we walked some way on, and then Albert drove home with us.*

Forest Lodge

After Albert had gone off stalking the Queen and her party drove eight miles up Glen Tilt as far as Forest Lodge, which was built in 1779 as part of the Duke's plans to turn the top of the glen into a deer forest. It was a simple building of two rooms, one for servants and the other for the gentry, with both rooms being linked by a castellated archway which crossed the glen track. The lodge was considerably enlarged a hundred years later. From here the Queen was able to observe a deer drive from the shelter of a nearby wood. Some 800 to 1,000 deer were herded and driven by the Atholl stalkers towards Albert's position, as Lady Canning observed in her diary:

> *. . . Then came a great drove of deer over the ridge & pouring down the hillside in one continuous stream. Some were very near the valley when something frightened them and made them turn about & scramble up the hill again.*

The immense herd was disturbed by the appearance of two men walking down the glen road, so that the Prince's sport that day was completely ruined. One of the 'intruders' was the Episcopal minister of Kilmaveonaig church, the Reverend Thomas Walker who lived in Middlebridge and he wrote to Lord Glenlyon to apologise:

Understanding that by my unlucky appearance in Glen Tilt last Thursday I was partly the means of turning the very fine drive of that day to the disappointment doubtless of the royal party and the consequent annoyance of your Lordship, I beg to express my deep regret that I should have been in any way the cause of the unfortunate circumstance.

Lord Glenlyon was furious that a shoot which had taken much time and trouble to organise had been spoiled, while the Prince was of the opinion that the minister should be encouraged to spend more time reading and preaching and less time 'trespassing' in the forest.

The Marquis of Breadalbane arrived on the Friday morning for a two-day stay, when he invited the royal couple to visit Taymouth Castle, but the invitation was declined. After lunch he accompanied the Queen and Lady Canning two miles beyond Forest Lodge to a stream called Allt a'Chrochaidh, where they crouched in a low, stone bothy as a sort of hiding place from which they could observe Prince Albert's shoot. From this vantage point a spectacular view is to be had of the corries that are part of the Beinn a'Ghlo mountain range, and it was in one of these where the Prince was shooting that afternoon. Beinn a'Ghlo covers a range of mountains over 3,000ft (915m) – Carn Liath, Braigh Coire Chruinn-bhalgain, Airgiod Bheinn and Carn nan Gabhar, with the highest being over 3,500ft (1,068m). There are twenty-eight corries in the range and according to William Scrope, the great sportsman:

These corries, though contiguous, are separated from each other by such high ridges that a person standing in one of them could not hear a shot fired in the next.

That evening Lord and Lady Glenlyon dined in Blair Castle as official guests of the royal couple, having earlier received the following invitation:

The Lord Steward is commanded by Her Majesty to invite the Lord and Lady Glenlyon to dinner this day Friday 20th Sep. 1844 at 8 o'clock.

The Glenlyons must have felt very strange at receiving a formal invitation to dine in their own home!

A Day in Glen Tilt

Saturday, September 21.
After breakfast Albert saw Lord Glenlyon, who proposed that he should go deer-stalking, and that I should follow him. At twenty minutes to eleven we drove off with Lady Canning for Glen Tilt. The day was glorious, and it would have been a pity to lose it, but it was a long, hard day's work, though extremely delightful and

enjoyable, and unlike anything I had ever done before. I should have enjoyed it still more had I been able to be with Albert the whole time.

We drove nearly to Peter Fraser's house, which is between the Marble Lodge and Forest Lodge. Here Albert and I walked about a little, and then Lady Canning and we mounted our ponies and set off on our journey, Lord Glenlyon leading my pony the whole way, Peter Fraser, the head keeper (a wonderfully active man), leading the way; Sandy and six other Highlanders carrying rifles and leading dogs, and the rear brought up by two ponies with our luncheon-box.

Saturday was another day spent in Glen Tilt, the Queen travelling by carriage as far as Clachglas, six miles up the glen and home for Peter Fraser. Others in the party included Lord Liverpool, Lord Wellesley, George Anson and Lady Canning. The 'wonderfully active' Peter Fraser, who had spent all his life in the glen, started working for the Atholl family as a stalker in 1830 and was appointed head stalker in 1839. His house was built at the start of the last century and still stands, near to a modern house, home to a present-day under keeper. Peter Fraser is reported to have spoken to Prince Albert and told him he 'had been thirty-seven years here and during that time I have not seen before so good a shot as you are'. It seems Peter Fraser was somewhat diplomatic, as by all accounts the Prince was not a very great shot.

Lawley, Albert's Jäger, was also there, carrying one of Albert's rifles; the other Albert slung over his right shoulder, to relieve Lawley. So we set off, and wound round and round the hill, which had the most picturesque effect imaginable. Such a splendid view all round, finer and more extensive the higher we went! The day was delightful but the sun very hot. We saw the highest point of Ben-y-Ghlo, which one can not see from below, and the distant range of hills we had seen from Tulloch was beautifully softened by the slightest haze. We saw Loch Vach. The road was very good, and as we ascended we had to speak in a whisper, as indeed we did almost all day, for fear of coming on deer unawares. The wind was, however, right, which is everything here for the deer. I wish we could have had Landseer with us to sketch our party, with the background, it was so pretty, as were also the various 'halts,' etc. If I only had had time to sketch them!

We stopped at the top of the Chrianan, whence you look down an immense height. It is here that the eagles sometimes sit. Albert got off and looked about in great admiration, and walked on a little, and then remounted his pony. We then went nearly to the top of Cairn Chlamain, and here we separated, Albert going off with Peter, Lawley, and two other keepers, to get 'a quiet shot,' as they call it; and Lady Canning, Lord Glenlyon, and I went up quite to the top, which is deep in moss. Here we sat down, and staid some time sketching the ponies below, Lord Glenlyon and Sandy remaining near us. The view was quite beautiful, nothing but mountains all around us, and the solitude, the complete solitude, very impressive. We saw the range of Mar Forest, and the inner range to the left, receding from us as we sat facing the hill, called Scarsach, where the counties of Perth, Aberdeen, and Inverness join. My pony was brought up for me, and we then descended this highest pinnacle, and proceeded on a level to meet Albert, whom I descried coming towards us. We met him shortly after; he had had bad luck I am sorry to say. We then sat down on the grass and had some luncheon; then I walked a little with Albert, and we got on our ponies.

Queen Victoria had a high opinion of Lawley, describing him as 'a very good man'. He gave up being a Jäger in 1848 through ill health and was appointed as a Page. Now, mounted on their ponies and guided by Peter Fraser, they rode up the peat road behind the house, quickly gaining another 500ft (153m) in height as the track rises steeply up beside Allt Craoinidh. Grianan Mor is a rocky outcrop high above the glen and below the 3,000ft (900m) mountain called Cairn a'Chlamain ('hill of the buzzard'), where the Queen stopped to sketch the scene whilst Albert went off to shoot. Looking north she could see An Scarsoch, a 3,000ft (900m) mountain where tradition has it that a cattle and horse fair was held on the summit and traces of an ancient stone causeway were found in the last century. Two miles to the west, on the summit of Carn an Fhidhleir, there is a large cairn which marks the meeting point of the three counties; Perthshire, Aberdeenshire and Inverness-shire. The Queen met up again with Albert lower down, when they had a picnic lunch.

As we went on toward home some deer were seen in Glen Chroime, which is called the 'Sanctum,' where it is supposed that there are a great many. Albert went off soon after this, and we remained on Sron a Chro for an hour, I am sure, as Lord Glenlyon said by so doing we should turn the deer on Albert, whereas if we went on we should disturb and spoil the whole thing. So we submitted. Albert looked like a little speck creeping about on an opposite hill. We saw four herds of deer, two of them close to us. It was a beautiful sight.

To prevent them from disturbing the deer, the Queen and her party stayed on the hilltops and moved to Sron a'Chro, a prominent rocky outcrop of about 2,500ft (763m) overlooking Glen Tilt, from where she had a bird's-eye view of Prince Albert, a 'little speck', in Glen Craoinidh and passed an hour observing the scene.

Meanwhile I saw the sun sinking gradually, and I got quite alarmed lest we should be benighted, and we called anxiously for Sandy, who had gone away for a moment, to give a signal to come back. We then began our descent, 'squinting' the hill, the ponies going as safely and securely as possible. As the sun went down the scenery became more and more beautiful, the sky crimson, golden-red, and blue, and the hills looking purple and lilac, most exquisite, till at length it set, and the hues grew softer in the sky and the outlines of the hills sharper. I never saw any thing so fine. It soon, however, grew very dark.

At length Albert met us, and he told me he had waited all the time for us, as he knew how anxious I should be. He had been very unlucky, and had lost his sport,

> *for the rifle would not go off just when he could have shot some fine harts; yet he was as merry and cheerful as if nothing had happened to disappoint him. We got down quite safely to the bridge; our ponies going most surely, though it was quite dusk when we were at the bottom of the hill. We walked to the Marble Lodge, and then got into the pony carriage and drove home by very bright moonlight, which made every thing look very lovely; but the road made one a little nervous. We saw a flight of ptarmigan, with their white wings, on the top of Sron a Chro; also plovers, grouse and pheasants. We were safely home by a quarter to eight.*

Yet again the Prince was dogged by bad luck – this time his rifle had jammed and he complained that he could not manage the bolt action. Dusk had fallen by the time the Queen had ridden down to the glen road and got into her carriage at Marble Lodge. On their way down the glen they found Lady Glenlyon and Lady Cocks, seated beside a makeshift camp fire with members of the Queen's bodyguard. Lord James Murray had caught a couple of dozen small trout, which they cooked over the fire and ate. The Queen thoroughly enjoyed these mountain excursions, which according to the *Illustrated London News* appeared to be one of her favourite pastimes:

> Had her Majesty been born and bred a mountaineer, she could not enter on them with more spirit. Wrapped in her plain shepherd's plaid, and equipped like a Highland gude wife, on her mountain pony, she leaves all state and following behind her, to breathe the pure air of the hills, and view from a vantage ground the splendid prospects which spread themselves on every side.

On each day of the following week Queen Victoria travelled up Glen Tilt, sometimes to be with Prince Albert for grouse shooting, at other times to view deer drives on one of the Beinn a'Ghlo mountains. At the end of his three-week stay Albert rewarded the keepers who had served him so well. Peter Fraser and Sandy McAra each received £50, while Jock McAra was given £15 and John Macpherson, Jock Robertson, John Stewart and Henry Robertson each got £10, with Donald Stewart receiving £5. One hundred pounds was left to be shared out amongst the under keepers, while the parish minister also was given £100 to administer to the poor of Blair Atholl.

On the morning of Thursday 26 September the Queen drove through the Pass of Killiecrankie to visit Mr Archibald Butter of Faskally and walk in the grounds of his mansion house. She sat on a rustic seat overlooking the Trooper's Den, where the first shot in the Battle of Killiecrankie was fired by Iain Ban Beag MacRath, killing a cavalry officer. She also visited the Soldier's Leap where Donald MacBean, a government soldier, fled for his life at the end of the battle – such was his fear that he cleared 18ft (5.4m) across the Garry gorge to safety on the other side.

Servants' Dance

The royal couple attended a servants' dance in the Horn Hall on the evening of Friday 27 September. The Horn Hall, now part of the main stairway in Blair Castle, was brilliantly lit up by lights on the horn chandeliers and the walls were decorated with firearms, swords, shields, spears and Lochaber axes. Many of the officers of the Atholl Highlanders joined in the reels and Lord James Murray performed the sword dance. At two o'clock the following morning a serious fire broke out in the kitchen chimney of the Factor's House and the service wing and the stables were partly destroyed. A sentry at the castle door raised the alarm and Captain Oswald and other Highlanders raced up to the house to rescue Lord and Lady Glenlyon and their son. They prevented the fire from spreading to the main building and saved all the horses in the stable.

Departure

Tuesday, October 1.

At a quarter past eight o'clock we started, and were very, very sorry to leave Blair and the dear Highlands! Every little trifle and spot I had become attached to; our life of quiet and liberty, every thing was so pleasant, and all the Highlanders and people who went with us I had got to like so much. Oh! the dear hills, it made me very sad to leave them behind.

The phrase 'our life of quiet and liberty' seems to imply that Queen Victoria was serenely oblivious of the pressures around her in organising her stay, and also of the presence of the press. Throughout her visit a number of journalists were in constant attendance and stayed at the inns in Blair Atholl and Bridge of Tilt, both of which they praised for their 'excellent accommodation'. The *Times* reporter was seen rising at five o'clock in the morning to obtain a good vantage point from which to observe the movements of the royal couple, while journalists from the *Morning Post, Morning Chronicle* and *Morning Herald* were equally tenacious in their coverage of the royal visit.

On the Tuesday of departure the royal pair rose even earlier than usual and the Queen planted three oak trees on the rise in front of the castle, which are still thriving beside the present-day car park. She also planted a deodara tree beside the Banvie. Prince Albert and the Princess Royal planted three Scotch firs and three pine trees in the field beside the main drive and one of them remains to this day.

Lord Glenlyon rode with us, and we went back exactly the same road we came – through Killiecrankie, Pitlochrie, saw Logierait etc. The battle of Killiecrankie was fought in a field to your left, as you come from Blair and before you come to the pass; and Lord Dundee was shot in a garden immediately above the field at Urrard (formerly called Kinrory), which belongs to Mr Stewart of Urrard; the Stewarts of Urrard used formerly to live on Craig Urrard. We reached Dunkeld at half past eleven. Mr Oswald and Mr Patrick Small Keir, with a detachment of Highlanders

Mid-nineteenth century view of Dunkeld from the Bridge. St Adamnan's Cottage is visible in front of the cathedral

were there. We drove up to the door of the cottage at Dunkeld and got out there. It is beautifully situated, and the cottage is very pretty, with a good view of the river from the windows. Craig-y-Barns is a fine rocky hill to the left as you drive from Blair.

Dunkeld

Escorted by a detachment of Scots Greys, Queen Victoria retraced her route of three weeks earlier, accompanied by Lord Glenlyon and Lord James Murray as far as Dunkeld. Here they went into St Adamnan's Cottage, a fairly large, bow-fronted house and at that time the family's temporary residence in the town, located in front of the cathedral and overlooking the river.

We walked to look at the beginning of the new house which the late Duke of Athole commenced, but which has been left unfinished, and also at a beautiful larch tree, the first that was brought to Scotland. I rode back on 'Arghait Bhean' for the last time, and took a sad leave of him and Sandy McAra. We walked into the ruins of the old cathedral and into that part which the late Duke fitted up for service, and where there is a fine monument of him. I should never have recognized the grounds of Dunkeld, so different did they look without the encampment. Beautiful as Dunkeld is, it does not approach the beauty and wildness of Blair.

Ruins of the lavish house begun by the 4th Duke of Atholl in 1828, but abandoned on his death two years later

It was a short walk from the town to the site of the new house started by the 4th Duke in 1828, as recorded in his journal:

June 29. Much employed all this week endeavouring to fix and stake the new site of house.

June 30. This day, by the mercy and favour of Providence, concluded my 72nd and tomorrow enter my 73rd year. Ran a furrow on the eastern, southern and western fronts on my new intended House, with a line from the Brick Buildings for the conveyance of materials.

This house was planned on a massive scale and would have become a magnificent Gothic mansion, containing a 96ft (29m) gallery, private chapel, a grand staircase and many fine mullioned windows. Duke John managed the Atholl Estate wisely and cautiously, built numerous roads, reorganised farms and planted millions of trees. He was a far-sighted man, but could not have foreseen that within thirty-five years the journey between Dunkeld and Blair Atholl would be quickly accomplished by the coming of the railway, thus removing the need for two large residences so close together. This project was, without doubt, his greatest mistake and the site chosen was most extraordinary, being in a hollow and, although well sheltered, any view of the River Tay was blocked by Bishop's Hill. It is difficult to conceive what induced him to embark on such an extravagant building programme so late in life, especially considering the ill health of his eldest son. The 4th Duke died two years later and by that time £30,000 had been spent out of a budget of £200,000 for the completed building. Work ceased immediately on his death, and it was an extravagant ruin when the Queen saw it in 1844.

The Queen rode back to the cathedral and was shown two of the five European larches which had been planted as seedlings in 1738. These were brought from the Tyrol and were some of the earliest to be planted in Scotland. The five seedlings thrived beside the Tay and were the larches for which Dunkeld became famous, being the source of many of the great larch plantings undertaken by the Atholl family. Only two had survived by the time of the Queen's visit and they were known as the 'parent larches'. One was cut down in 1906, but the other survives to this day and is over 100ft (30m) tall. Here the Queen said goodbye to Sandy McAra and Airgiod Bheinn, the faithful pony which had served her so well and which she had come to trust. He was named after one of the Beinn a'Ghlo peaks and was presented to the Queen in 1847. Inside the cathedral the Queen saw the immense marble statue of Planter John, the 4th Duke of Atholl, of whom she had heard so much.

After twelve o'clock we set off again, and to our astonishment, Lord Glenlyon insisted upon riding with us to Dundee which is 50 miles from Blair! Captain J. Murray also rode with us from Dunkeld. It made me feel sad to see the country becoming flatter and flatter. There was a great crowd at Cupar Angus and at Dundee a still larger one, and on the pier the crush was very great.

We took leave of Lord Glenlyon with real regret, and he seemed quite unhappy at our going. No one could be more zealous or kinder than he was.

Having marched to Dunkeld the previous day, a detachment of Atholl Highlanders commanded by Captain Oswald escorted the royal cavalcade to the edge of the town. Lord Glenlyon escorted them on horseback all the way to Dundee, not arriving back at Blair Castle until five o'clock the following morning, having covered some 120 miles.

Within a week of leaving Blair Castle, Lady Cocks wrote to Lady Glenlyon and with some humour regarding bare-kneed pipers expressed her gratitude:

*. . . for all your kindness to us during the very happy time we spent at Blair. It was scarcely ever possible to say all one would wish at the last moment, but we did not take leave of you without many regrets and we shall always enjoy the thought of the time we spent in your lovely country – you were all so very good to us. I assure you that on the steamer we could talk of nothing but Blair and all connected with it, and whatever way the conversation began, it always ended there. I never saw the Queen in a greater state of enthusiasm about any Place. She said she was quite low at bidding farewell to the Hills and to you all. She was wonderfully well during our rough voyage and **the** subject furnished conversation for the whole time for it was one in which we all sympathised.*

Everything was talked over, from Ben-y-Glo to Peter Fraser, and downwards. I can scarcely believe that it was only a week yesterday since we took leave of you, having gone *through so many changes of scene since then – It was very tantalising to hurry away from Dunkeld as we did. You can imagine my delight at seeing Sandy's honest face and it was quite an unexpected pleasure, for I did not know he was to be there and I had looked out for him in vain, in the morning at Blair. We are all very anxious to hear that Ld. Glenlyon did not suffer from his long ride – Charlotte promised to let me know when she heard from you. We took a very hurried leave of him at Dundee while we were on the verge of being pushed into the water, if he had not kindly taken charge of me I should soon have been squeezed into a scon, but as for thanks I attempted none, they would have been unheard in such a scene of confusion. To say **how** I miss the BagPipes, kilts and oatmeal Porridge is impossible – the latter can be supplied and we have sent to Scotland for Oatmeal, but I must make up my mind to dispense with kilts and Pipers. I assure you that at Windsor, when Mackay was waiting at dinner I looked at his bare knees with an interest which they had never inspired before . . . . The last thing the Queen said to me was how she missed the Hills, and quite envied me the sight of those about us. I must confess that I was very glad not to be obliged to remain at Windsor. Blair spoilt me for the grand & dull routine of a Court Life, and I was much more disposed to enjoy the liberty of my own Home.*

The three-week royal stay in Blair Castle was a great success: the Queen's health had much improved and Prince Albert enjoyed some excellent sport. Queen Victoria obviously enjoyed the great contrast with her court life at Windsor and yet, despite the pleasure that she gained from the Atholl countryside and its people, it was to be seventeen years before she returned, and then only for a fleeting visit.

On 5 November 1845 Lady Glenlyon wrote to the Queen, having heard that a position as a Lady in Waiting had become vacant, and offered her services as a successor. The Queen replied within a few days to say that the post had been filled, and her letter continues:

. . . I am however pleased to know for the future that you are amongst those who have expressed a desire to belong to my Household. The return of autumn brought forcibly to our minds the recollection of the pleasant time we spent at Blair Athole last year . . .

Mistress of the Robes

In March 1852 Lady Glenlyon, by then the 6th Duchess of Atholl, was offered the post of Mistress of the Robes by the government. Lord Derby stated that its acceptance would in no way bind the Duke of Atholl, who was pledged to Sir Robert Peel's party, to his own. The Queen was delighted with this news, as her letter to the Duchess reveals:

As the Duchess of Sutherland has resigned her office of Mistress of the Robes (which is customary at change of Government) I am desirous of appointing you as her successor. Remembering as I do your wish to be about my person – which you expressed to me some time ago, I hope that you will have no difficulty in accepting this office the duties of which you will not find arduous and which it would afford me much pleasure to see filled by you.

In her reply Duchess Anne wrote that she had great pleasure in accepting the post of Mistress of the Robes and hoped she would fill it to the Queen's satisfaction. Queen Victoria was delighted by the acceptance, as is demonstrated by her letter of 20 March 1852:

My Dear Duchess

Most truly do I congratulate you and the Duke on your situation as Mistress of the Robes. No appointment could give me more satisfaction. I trust it will afford me the great pleasure of seeing you a great deal more than I have hitherto done.
With affectionate regard
My dear Duchess

Your very sincere friend

Victoria

The relationship between Duchess Anne and Queen Victoria was further strengthened, but within a year the government fell and she had to resign the office of Mistress of the Robes. The Queen's letter to the Duchess recorded her sorrow as she wrote:

You have been so amicable, so zealous and obliging while you held that position that I shall deeply regret parting with you.

A year later Duchess Anne accepted the Queen's appointment as one of her Ladies of the Bedchamber.

CHAPTER THREE

1861
A Great Expedition

BLAIR ATHOLL,
9 OCTOBER

When Queen Victoria and Prince Albert reached Deeside in September 1848 they immediately fell in love with the area, as the Queen recorded in her diary:

> *It was so clear and so solitary, it did one good as one gazed around; and the pure mountain air was most refreshing. All seemed to breathe freedom and peace, and to make one forget the world and its sad turmoils.*

Balmoral

The first priority was to obtain the freehold of Balmoral, pull down the old castle and build a larger one nearby. This was necessary in order to accommodate the ever-increasing royal family and household – equerries, ladies in waiting, secretaries, and guest rooms for visiting ministers of the government. By 1849 Queen Victoria and Prince Albert had six children, with Princess Victoria, the eldest, being then eight years old and so more rooms were required for them and their nurses and governesses. Negotiations to buy the freehold were put in hand without delay, and in 1852 the Balmoral Estate passed into royal hands. Three years later the new Balmoral Castle was virtually ready and was occupied for the first time, so at last, after thirteen years, Queen Victoria achieved her dream of having her own home in the Highlands.

Travelling around Scotland had become much easier. Gone were the long stays in the stately homes of dukes and lords and other parts of the Highlands had become more accessible. The Court at Windsor provided all the pomp and ceremony that the Queen required and she still hankered for the simplicity of life that she had experienced in Atholl. In 1861 three 'Great Expeditions' were planned, the third of these taking her right through the heart of part of her favourite countryside. General Sir Charles Grey was put in charge of all the arrangements and the choice of routes for these excursions. He became Private Secretary to Prince Albert in 1846 and in 1861 was appointed as Private Secretary to the Queen. It was he who organised the security arrangements at Balmoral, and British troops were stationed there for the first time

'. . . and in a few minutes more were at the door of the old castle' – Queen Victoria

The Royal Family at Osborne in 1857, left to right: *Prince Alfred (13); Prince Albert; Princess Helena (11); Princess Alice (14); Prince Arthur (7); Princess Beatrice (6 months); Queen Victoria; Princess Victoria (17); Princess Louise (9); Prince Leopold (4); Prince Albert Edward (16).*

in 1861. He died in 1870, highly esteemed by the Queen who wrote of him: 'His loss grieved me deeply.'

The day before the start of the third Expedition, General Grey went on ahead to reconnoitre the route and stayed the night of 7 October at the Bridge of Tilt Hotel, hoping to meet Duchess Anne to discuss his arrangements. She, however, was away at the time, so he wrote her a lengthy letter and continued on to Dalwhinnie, as he was covering the route in reverse and planned to meet up with the royal party in Glen Feshie.

His letter was extremely detailed and reads as follows:

*I was **very** sorry not to find you at home, both because it wd. have been a great pleasure to see you, & because it is easier to explain by word of mouth what makes a long story, & a confused one on paper.*

*I am going on to Dalwhinnie to sleep – & it is in the **strictest confidence** I tell you, that it is in order to make arrangements for the Queen's sleeping there tomorrow. I was ordered by H.M. to call on you on my way, & explain, as I did in Invermark to Lord Dalhousie without offering to stop. It is her pleasure to preserve a strict incognito, as far as that is possible – or at all events not to let it be known who it is till she is gone by and that she may avoid all troublesome demonstrating.*

If there is nobody with you she would call at the Castle & stop ½ an hour – but would not lunch – She declares that a hot luncheon or one in a house, on such occasions, makes her quite ill afterwards. In fact she would rather lunch by the Tilt on her way up the glen, & at any hour, however late, than sit down to her luncheon, that often was cooked, in a regular way, & at the regular hour.

*Her plans then are as follows: to leave Balmoral tomorrow at ½ past 8 & cross to Glen Feshie. I meet her with carriages near Invereshie shooting huts & she will sleep at Dalwhinnie. The next day, Wednesday, she proposes driving up to the Forest Lodge in Glen Tilt, calling at the castle on the way up, & there taking her ponies again for the Bynack, where her carriages meet her to take her home. If there is anybody with you, perhaps you could meet her somewhere up the glen so that she need not stop at the castle. You know the **complexion** Her Majesty puts on these occasions also that she is **somewhat** of a Dowdy in appearance – & that one is not anxious to parade one's Sovereign in public.*

The three points H.M. insisted upon with me were:

1. to explain to you & the Duke why she did not propose to pay you a regular visit.

2. to preserve her incognito.

3. to avoid luncheon indoors – tho' she cd. be ready to have a cup of tea, or (I am afraid she said) a glass of whisky toddy!

P.S. For heaven's sake dont let H.M.'s identity ooze out. I pledged myself you would not.

On Tuesday 8 October the royal party drove out from Balmoral on a dull and overcast morning which threatened rain. Princess Alice, (Victoria's third child, born in 1843 and great grandmother of Prince Philip), was accompanied by her fiancé, Prince Louis of Hesse

Darmstadt. Also in the party were John Grant, the Queen's head ghillie, John Brown and Lady Churchill. They followed a route through Glen Feshie, past Loch Insh and then by the gaunt ruins of Ruthven Barracks, to arrive at what is now the Loch Ericht hotel in Dalwhinnie in time for supper. This proved more than a little disappointing, as the Queen recorded in her diary:

> *. . . but, unfortunately, there was hardly any thing to eat, and there was only tea, and two miserable starved Highland chickens, without any potatoes! No pudding, and no **fun**; . . .*

This episode underlines the problems of making no formal arrangements in advance, but the Queen seemed to enjoy the uncertainty of it all and of not knowing what lay ahead. At any event, on this occasion the accommodation seemed to be satisfactory.

Drumochter

> *Wednesday, October 9.*
> *We drove as we did yesterday. Fine and very wild scenery, high, wild hills, and no habitations. We went by the Pass of Drumouchter, with fine hills on both sides and in front of us; passed between two, the one on our left called the Boar of Badenoch, and that on the right The Athole Sow. The Pass of Drumouchter separates Perthshire from Inverness-shire.*

Drumochter marks the Perth/Inverness County March and here, at a height of just over 1,500ft (450m) the royal party left Badenoch, in those days part of the Duke of Gordon's estate and entered the land of Atholl. This great pass through the Grampian Mountains was described in an 1843 *Guide to the Highlands* as:

> The bleak and moorish wilds where nought but stunted grass and heather, dark swamp, impetuous torrents, grey rocks and frowning heights and precipices are to be seen. The mountains also are heavy and seem to be broken into great detached mounds.

March stones marked the county boundary in the eighteenth century, with 'A' for Atholl on one side and 'B' for Badenoch on the other, and one stood in such a way 'that if you were to empty a pail of water upon the top of it, part would run to the County of Inverness and part of it to the County of Perth.' Here in Queen Victoria's time there was a toll house, which in 1830 was granted a licence 'to retail spirits and ale', doubtless essential in this isolated spot even in summer. The Boar of Badenoch, a 2,400ft (732m) mountain and the Sow of Atholl, at 2,600ft (793m), are both to the right of the road coming south, rather than on each side as described by the Queen.

> *Again, a little farther on, we came to Loch Garry, which is very beautiful – but the mist covered the farthest hills, and the extreme distance was clouded. There is a small shooting lodge or farm, charmingly situated, looking up the glen on both*

'. . . then went to the Factor's House, still higher up . . .' – Queen Victoria

One of the twenty statues in Hercules Garden, Blair Castle

Willie Duff, who was kept prisoner in the tent all night in 1844

'. . . the river Tilt gushing and winding over stones and slates . . .' – Queen Victoria (1844)

Blair Atholl church, where the royal couple attended service on the first Sunday in 1844

Balmoral Castle

Dalnacardoch Lodge, formerly an inn on the King's Road. The stone plaque is beside the entrance porch

sides, and with the loch in front: we did not hear to whom it belonged. We passed
many drovers, without their herds and flocks, returning, Grant told us, from Falkirk.

Loch Garry is quite a small loch, three miles long and easily seen from the A9. Now it is a reservoir for hydro-electricity and water from it is pumped through a huge underground tunnel to Loch Errochty. In the middle of the seventeenth century a battle took place here between a royalist army led by Lieutenant General Middleton, with 1,200 foot soldiers supported by 800 cavalry who had marched over from Rannoch, against a body of Cromwellian troops led by Colonel Morgan, who had progressed south from Ruthven. As the royalists retreated along the narrow defile beside Loch Garry the cavalry became separated from the foot soldiers, and were routed by the English troops. Many of the royalists escaped by dismounting and taking to their heels, but the English gained a rich prize of over 300 horses. This clash hardly ranks as a great set-piece engagement, yet its effect on the royalist cause was disastrous, as it seriously weakened their cavalry strength.

Until the coming of the military road, Dalnaspidal was a place of summer pasture, but the people then saw opportunities to be gained from the passing traffic. A public house was opened and drovers were permitted to graze their livestock, provided they paid for the pasture. The small shooting lodge noted by Queen Victoria was later replaced by a much larger house early this century. By the 1860s much of General Wade's military road had been bypassed and improved, but the Queen's route passed close by the site of a great feast held in 1729 to celebrate the completion of the road between Perth and Inverness. Here, beside the Oxbridge, according to Wade:

> *. . . there were four (oxen) roasting at the same time in great order and solemnity. We*
> *dined in a tent pitched for that purpose; the beef was excellent . . . and after three hours'*
> *stay, took leave of our Benefactors the Highwaymen and arrived at the Hutt*
> *(Dalnacardoch) before it was dark.*

A few miles down the road the royal party passed the Wade Stone, an 8ft (2.4m) high standing stone dated 1729. Tradition has it that General Wade placed a guinea on the top and returned a year later to find it still there.

We had one very heavy shower after Loch Garry, and before we came to the
Dalnacardoch Inn, 13 miles from Dalwhinnie. The road goes beside the Garry. The
country for a time became flatter, but was a good deal cultivated. At Dalnacardoch
Inn there was a suspicion and expectation of our arrival. Four horses with smart
*postillions were in waiting; but on General Grey's saying that this was **not** the party,*
but the one for whom only two horses had been ordered, a shabby pair of horses
were put in, a shabby driver driving from the box (as throughout this journey), and
off we started.

Dalnacardoch was the next change-house on the road, ten miles from Blair Castle. Having been firmly instructed not to let the Queen's identity 'ooze out', General Grey was horrified to discover that news of her arrival in the area had leaked out at Dalnacardoch and in an attempt to continue the deception he refused the especially smart horses provided by saying they were not for his party, so that indifferent animals were used for the remainder of the journey to Blair Castle.

Dalnacardoch was at an important junction on the military road, and General Wade had his 'hutt' or headquarters here when he was supervising the construction of this part of the road. This was the forerunner of the inn built in 1732 and enlarged forty years later. The coming of the railway diverted much of the traffic from the road, and the inn closed in 1865. However, there is a permanent reminder of its former use to be seen on a stone plaque near the front door which bears the inscription 'AD 1774. Rest a little while' in Latin, English and Gaelic. In the 1860s a substantial farm was attached to the inn which pastured 1,000 sheep and sixteen cattle and they grew oats, barley, turnips and potatoes on sixty acres of arable land.

> *The Garry is very fine, rolling along over large stones – like the Quoich and the Fishie, and forming perpetual falls, with birch and mountain ash growing down to the water's edge. We had some more heavy showers. A few miles from Dalnacardoch the Duke of Athole (in his kilt and shooting-jacket, as usual) met us on a pretty little chestnut pony, and rode the whole time near the carriage. He said there were vague suspicions and rumors of our coming, but he had told no one any thing. There was again a shower, but it cleared when we came in sight of Ben-y-Ghlo, and the splendid Pass of Killiecrankie, which with the birch all golden – not, as on Deeside, bereft of leaves – looked very beautiful.*

Lord Glenlyon, now the 6th Duke of Atholl, had set off from Blair Castle at ten o'clock and met the royal party somewhere near the Dalnamein Bridge, close to another of his shooting lodges. This single arched stone bridge with a 28ft (8.6m) span is a fine example of a Wade bridge and was in use until the 1920s, when this section of the road was bypassed. It is still standing and is yet another example of his superb engineering carried out over 260 years ago.

Blair Castle

> *We passed by the Bruar, and the road to the Falls of Bruar, but could not stop. The Duke took us through a new approach, which is extremely pretty, but near which, I cannot help regretting, the railroad will come, as well as along the road by which we drove through the Pass of Drumouchter. The Duke has made great improvements, and the path looked beautiful, surrounded as it is by hills; and the foliage still full, though in all its autumn tints – the whole being lit up with bright sunshine. We drove through an avenue, and in a few minutes more were at the door of the old castle.*

Within two miles of the castle the Duke guided the party off the main road and along the West Drive, very close to the route of the railway line which was to open two years later. Near the castle the drive descends gently through a tree-lined avenue, overlooked by the

The 6th Duke of Atholl met the party near Dalnamein Bridge, built in the 1720s

'Whim', higher up the hillside. This folly, described as a 'sham castle backed with trees', was erected in 1762 when the 2nd Duke was extending the castle grounds. When he told the parish minister he was at a loss as to what to call it, the Rev Stewart replied that it would be difficult, as it was but a 'whim'.

A thousand recollections of seventeen years ago crowded upon me – all seemed so familiar again! No one there except the dear Duchess, who stood at the door, and whom I warmly embraced; and Miss MacGregor. How well I recognized the hall, with all the sporting trophies; and the staircase, which we went up at once. The Duchess took us to a room which I recognized immediately as the one where Lady Canning lived. There we took off our things – then went to look at the old and really very handsome rooms in which we had lived – the one in which Vicky had slept in two chairs, then not four years old! In the dining-room we took some coffee,

> *which was most welcome; and then we looked at all the stags horns put up in one of the corridors below; saw the Duke's pet dog, a smooth-haired black terrier, very fat . . .*

It was indeed seventeen years since Victoria and Albert's last visit, and she was happy and delighted to be back in such familiar surroundings. Though she saw Duchess Anne regularly through her duties as a Lady of the Bedchamber, she was nonetheless overjoyed at seeing her again in her own home. She also met Miss Amelia MacGregor for the first time and over the years to come a very special relationship developed between them. Born in 1829, Amelia was the daughter of Lady Elizabeth Murray MacGregor, eighth child of the 4th Duke, and therefore a cousin to the 6th Duke. After the death of her brother, Sir John Murray MacGregor, in 1851, she took up permanent residence with the Atholl family and became the constant companion of Duchess Anne, accompanying her on all her travels, both at home and abroad.

Little had changed at the castle, and Duchess Anne conducted her royal guests through the Horn Hall and up the main staircase to the room on the first floor that Lady Canning had used in 1844, now almost certainly known as the Blue Room. After this they revisited their own old rooms and memories of those happy three weeks of 1844 came flooding back. After coffee, rather than whisky, in the dining room, (thus allaying General Grey's fears!) the royal party set off again.

Travelling through Glen Tilt

> *. . . and then got into the carriage, a very peculiar one, viz., a **boat** – a mere boat (which is very light), put on four wheels, drawn by a pair of horses with a postillion. Into this we four got, with the Duke and Duchess and the dog – Lady Churchill, General Grey, and Miss MacGregor going in another carriage, with our two servants on the box, to whom all this was new and a great treat. The morning was beautiful. It was half past twelve. We drove up by the avenue and about a favourite walk of ours in '44, passed through the gate, and came on to Glen Tilt, which is most striking, the road winding along first on one side of the Tilt, and then on the other; the fine high hills rising very abruptly from each side of the rapid, rocky, stony River Tilt – the trees, chiefly birch and alder, overhanging the water.*

The Queen was obviously greatly intrigued by the unusual carriage which was to convey her up Glen Tilt. They drove up the avenue round Diana's Grove, one of her favourite walks in 1844, and followed the old military road to Tibby's Lodge, which was built at the time of the construction of the military road and named after a gatekeeper, Tibby Cameron. The archway was put up soon afterwards and when the military road was re-routed in 1752 a gate was erected here. Tibby's Lodge was at the entrance to Glen Tilt but by 1880 was falling into disrepair, so it was pulled down and the East Lodge was built across the road four years later. Undoubtedly Glen Tilt was Queen Victoria's favourite glen in Atholl, and she was enthusiastic at the prospect of travelling right through it on her journey back to Balmoral.

The boat carriage in front of Blair Castle, by Richard Leitch (R L 19655)

Thomas Pennant, the famous eighteenth-century traveller, passed through the glen nearly a hundred years earlier and gives a vivid description of how it was in 1769:

> . . . *Glen Tilt, famous in old times for producing the most hardy warriors; is a narrow glen several miles in length, bounded on each side by mountains of an amazing height; on the South is the great hill of Ben y glo, whose base is thirty-five miles in circumference, and whose summit towers far above the others. The sides of many of these mountains is covered with fine verdure, and are excellent sheep-walks: but entirely woodless. The road is the most dangerous and the most horrible I ever travelled: a narrow path, so rugged that our horses often were obliged to cross their legs, in order to pick a secure place for their feet; while, at a considerable and precipitous depth beneath, roared a black torrent, rolling through a bed of rock, solid in every part but where the Tilt had worn its antient way. Salmon force their passage even as high as this dreary stream, in spite of the distance from the sea, and the difficulties they have to encounter.*

The royal party followed the 'Duke's Drive', completed in 1805 as the main way up the glen. It first crosses the Tilt by the Cumhann Leum Bridge and then re-crosses it three miles further on by Gow's Bridge, near the marble quarry.

We passed the Marble Lodge in which one of the keepers live, and came to Forest Lodge, where the road for carriages ends, and the glen widens. There were four ponies, which had passed the night at Bainoch or Beynoch (a shooting 'shiel' of Lord Fife's). They came over this morning, but, poor beasts, without having had any corn! Forest Lodge is eight miles from Blair. There we took leave of the dear Duchess, and saw old Peter Fraser, the former head keeper there, now walking with the aid of two sticks! The Duke's keepers were there, his pipers, and a gentleman staying on a visit with him.

Forest Lodge marked the end of the carriage road, and here the royal party mounted riding ponies which had been sent from Bynack Lodge on Lord Fife's estate in Aberdeenshire, over ten miles distant on the route to Balmoral. The Queen bade her farewells to the Duchess and met Peter Fraser, her guide in 1844, now an old man, crippled with arthritis, walking with the help of sticks.

It was barely two o'clock when we started, we got on our ponies, the Duke and his men (twelve altogether) on foot – Sandy McAra, now head keeper, grown old and gray, and two pipers, preceded us, the two latter playing alternately the whole time, which had a most cheerful effect. The wild strains sounded so softly amid these noble hills; and our caravan winding along – our people and the Duke's all in kilts, and the ponies, made altogether a most picturesque scene. One of the Duke's keepers, Donald Macbeath, is a Guardsman, and was in the Crimea. He is a celebrated marksman, and a fine-looking man, as all the Duke's men are. For some little time it was easy riding, but soon we came to a rougher path, more on the 'brae' of the hill, where the pony required to be led, which I always have done, either when it is at all rough or bad, or when the pony has to be got on faster.

Donald Macbeath

Sandy McAra, now head keeper, led the way from Forest Lodge, and among the twelve estate keepers was Donald Macbeath. It is hardly surprising that the Queen picked him out, as he was a man of great presence with a fine war record. Several generations of his family lived in Clach-Glas in Glen Tilt and his grandfather, Archibald Macbeath, had served under Lord George Murray in 1745.

Donald Macbeath was born in 1831 at Rienakyllich, a farm under the east shoulder of Carn Liath and enlisted in the Scots Fusilier Guards in 1851. He was promoted to corporal and embarked with the regiment for the Crimea in 1854. He took part in the battle of the Alma where his regiment, 'by its heroic conduct in circumstances of great difficulty, prevented what might have been a serious disaster.' After this he was promoted to sergeant and, as he was the best shot, was appointed the Brigade Sharpshooter. Because of this, he was constantly engaged in advance of his own trenches. He saw action at Balaclava and Inkerman, where he had no less than fourteen bullet holes in his clothes, but was himself unharmed. Writing to his father, who lived in Middlebridge above Blair Atholl, on 29 January 1855 shortly before the battle of Sebastopol, he recorded his thoughts and feelings:

The only thing I want now is to get home and see what is going on and see my friends once more.

God was favourable to me and saved my life. Many a time I have been surrounded with russians but I paced them and got clean away without a scratch.

In another letter of 21 April 1855 he wrote:

I was never better in all my life. I am strong as a horse and as fat as a bullock. Our clothing is never off. We lay with our arms and accoutrements on and sometimes turn out Between 2 & 3 in the morning for fear of an attack. There is twelve months now since I had my clothes off in the time.

On 6 September 1855 Donald rescued a sentry, Private Thomas Sankey, who had been badly wounded in advance of a covering party. Donald found himself in the Russian trenches and, under appalling conditions, carried the sentry to safety on his back. The citation for a medal was drawn up by Major Gerald Goodlake, Coldstream Guards, and read as follows:

Date of act of Bravery 6th Sept. 1855

For having when in the right advanced sap in front of the Redan, volunteered to go out and look for the body of Captain Buckley, Sco. Fus. Guards who was supposed to be wounded – after seeing him safely carried in by Sergeant Craig and a drummer – he went in search of Thomas Sankey who was dangerously wounded and carried him into the advanced sap – on his back under a tremendous fire of grape and small arms.

Sergeant Macbeath late of the Scots Fusilier Guards volunteered for the sharp shooters of the Brigade of Guards in October 1854 – served with them for 42 days – displaying at all times great courage and coolness especially on 28th October 1854 on the occasion of the surprise of a picquet of the enemy in November, at the bottom of the Windmill Ravine.

Donald Macbeath was awarded the medal of Distinguished Conduct in the Field, although there were many who believed he merited the Victoria Cross for his incredible bravery. He was discharged from the army in November 1855 and in his commendation to the Duke of Atholl, dated 31 May 1858, his commanding officer wrote:

During the latter part of the campaign I had several opportunities of observing and admiring his courage and bravery. He was always the first to volunteer when anything was wanted – and at all times showed such a disinterest to himself and devotion to his country which proved him to be endowed with that true courage necessary in a British soldier.

When he returned to Atholl the Duke employed him as a deerstalker in Glen Tilt, and when Sandy McAra retired as head keeper in 1864 Donald was appointed in his place. Later he became Sergeant Major of the Atholl Highlanders and was known as the 'father of the regiment'.

The steepest part of this section of the route, as mentioned in the Queen's diary, is some four miles beyond Forest Lodge, where it rises quickly to reach a turning off to the left. Called the Dunmore Walk, this climbs steeply out of the glen, passing the shieling of Ruigh Allt Mhcann, amongst several others, before dropping into Glen Tarf. The Glen Tilt road descends again, and within half a mile reaches Dail a'Chruineachd.

> *The Duke walked near me the greater part of the time, amusingly saying, in reference to former times, that he did not offer to lead me, as he knew I had no confidence in him. I replied, laughingly, 'Oh no, only I like best being led by the person I am accustomed to.'*
>
> *At length, about three, we stopped and lunched at a place called Dalcronachie, looking up a glen toward Loch Loch, on a high bank overhanging the Tilt. Looking back, the view was very fine; so, while the things were being unpacked for lunch, we sketched. We brought our own luncheon, and the remainder was, as usual, given to the men, but this time there were a great many to feed.*

Sixteenth-Century Royal Hunt

The royal party halted on a flat haugh of land opposite the confluence of the Lochain Burn with the Tilt and the Queen was told of an earlier royal event which took place across the river in 1529. Then, King James V of Scotland, accompanied by his mother Queen Margaret and the Pope's ambassador, stayed there for three days to take part in a gigantic hunt. John, the 3rd Stewart Earl of Atholl, gathered together all his men to form a huge circle and slowly, over many days, they drove all the deer in the area towards this spot in Glen Tilt, where at great expense he had built a temporary palace to accommodate his distinguished guests.

In the middle of a meadow stood the specially constructed palace of green timber with a block house, the height of three houses, at each corner. Floors were laid with turf, reeds and flowers, the walls were covered with fine tapestries and embroidered silks, and the whole was 'lighted up with fine glass windows in all pairts.' The way in was across a drawbridge over a moat stocked with salmon, trout, perch, pike and eels. The entertainment was equally lavish, with a great variety of food, drinks and other delicacies provided. For drinks there was ale, beer, red and white wine, malmsey, hippocras and aqua vitae. A great supply of meats was supplied, including beef, mutton, lamb, veal, venison, goose, grice, capon, rabbit, swan, partridge, plover, duck, drake, peacock, blackcock, grouse and capercaillie.

During the hunt 200 deer, a wolf, a fox and several wild cats were killed. Such was his determination to impress his guests, it was said that the cost to the Earl was £1,000 a day. The ambassador was amazed to find such excellence and luxury in so remote a spot, but was utterly dumbfounded when he saw the Highlanders set fire to the building when the festivities ended. 'Such is the constant practice of our Highlanders,' said the King, 'that however well they may have lodged over the night, they always burn their lodgings before they leave it.' It is difficult to imagine a more costly, yet more effective, way of impressing prestigious guests!

Mary Queen of Scots

The Lochain Burn flows out of Loch Loch and, although mentioned by Queen Victoria, it is three miles away and out of sight of the Glen Tilt road. It is a beautiful loch, in the shape of a fiddle – at one point the two sides almost meet and that is where it is possible to wade across. This accounts for its name, as there appear to be two lochs.

This was the site of another spectacular event in Atholl, when Mary Queen of Scots attended a huge hunt at the south end of the loch in 1564. Again, hundreds of Highlanders were employed in driving the deer for miles around to a given spot, where the Queen was waiting on a hillock now called Tom nan Ban Righ (Queen's Hillock). An account of this was given by William Barclay, one of the Queen's party:

> Two thousand Highlanders were employed to drive deer to the hunting ground, from the hills of Atholl, Badenoch, Mar and Muray and in less than two months they had collected 2,000 red deer, besides roes and fallow deer. The royal party were in Glen Loch, where they had encamped on the shore of Loch Loch, when all the deer were brought to them. The Queen ordered one of the dogs to be let loose upon a wolf and the leading stag, being frightened, took flight and the 2,000 deer followed right where the main body of the Highlanders were. All they could do was throw themselves flat on the ground and two or three were killed and several wounded. That day 360 deer, five wolves and some roes were killed.

It was three o'clock by the time the party sat down to lunch at Dail a'Chruineachd, opposite the old ford across the river and beside the building called Bothan Dail a'Chruineachd, now a ruin. It was built and thatched with heather in 1792 by eight men in three weeks.

Falls of Tarf

> After luncheon we set off again. I walked a few paces; but, as it was very wet, and the road very rough, by Albert's desire I got on again. A very few minutes brought us to the celebrated ford of the Tarff (Poll Tarff it is called), which is very deep, and, after heavy rain, almost impassable. The Duke offered to lead the pony on one side, and talked of Sandy for the other side, but I asked for Brown (whom I have far the most confidence in) to lead the pony, the Duke taking hold of it (as he did frequently) on the other side.

Sandy McAra, the guide, and the two pipers went first, playing all the time. To all appearances the ford of the Tarff was not deeper than the other fords, but once in it the men were above their knees – and suddenly in the middle, where the current, from the fine, high, full falls, is very strong, it was nearly up to the men's waists. Here Sandy returned, and I said to the Duke (which he afterwards joked with Sandy about) that I thought he (Sandy) had better take the Duke's place; he did so, and we came very well through, all the others following, the men chiefly wading – Albert (close behind me) and the others riding through – and some of our people coming over double on the ponies. General Grey had little Peter Robertson up behind him.

After a further mile the cavalcade arrived at the Falls of Tarf, where the River Tarf joins the Tilt. The Tarf is ten miles in length and drains the mountains that form the watershed along the county boundary of Perthshire with Aberdeenshire and Inverness-shire. The falls are spectacular in times of spate, when the water plunges several hundred feet from the plateau above. At times like this, the crossing is extremely dangerous. In the past Glen folk returning from Braemar sometimes lost part of their load in the middle of the river, which could be chest deep. In 1822 the nearest shooting lodge, Fealar, was burgled and eighteen bottles of claret, porter, hams and other items were either drunk, eaten or removed. The thieves attempted to cross the ford, and in so doing lost a horse as the water was so deep and turbulent. A single-arched stone bridge was built here in 1770, but was taken down in 1819 in an attempt to deter travellers from using the glen. It remained without a bridge for nearly seventy years until 1886, when the Bedford suspension bridge was erected by public subscription in memory of a student, Francis John Bedford, who had drowned seven years earlier while attempting the crossing.

Charles Stewart guided the party through the ford followed by the two pipers, John Macpherson and Aeneas Rose, who continued to play despite the water being up to their waists. John Macpherson had piped for the sword dance performed at Dunkeld in 1842, and Aeneas Rose succeeded him as Pipe Major to the Atholl Highlanders in 1870. He was a native of Badenoch, who entered the Duke's service in 1850 and later became Master of the Dunkeld otter hounds.

The road after this became almost precipitous, and, indeed, very unpleasant to ride; but being wet, and difficult to walk, we ladies rode, Albert walking the greater part of the time. Only once, for a very few steps, I had to get off, as the pony could hardly keep footing. As it was, Brown constantly could not walk next to the pony, but had to scramble below, or pull it after him. The Duke was indefatigable. The Tilt becomes narrower and narrower till its first source is almost invisible. The Tarff flows into the Tilt about two miles or more beyond the falls.

This stretch of the road was the part mentioned in Thomas Pennant's narrative – 'where our horses were often obliged to cross their legs' – and from here on to the watershed it is little more than a footpath which winds along the hillside, in many places above a steep gorge. Queen Victoria was not alone in being confused about the source of the River Tilt, which does not flow out of Loch Tilt on the watershed but two miles lower down at the confluence of two smaller rivers, Allt Garbh Buidh and Allt Feith Lair, half a mile above the falls.

We emerged from the pass upon an open valley, with less high hills and with the hills of Braemar before us. We crossed the Bainoch or Bynack, quite a small stream, and when we came to the 'County March' – where Perth and Aberdeen join – we halted. The Duke gave Albert and me some whisky to drink out of an old silver flask of his own, and then made a short speech proposing my health, expressing the pleasure with which he and all had received me at Blair, and hoping that I would return as often as I liked, and that I should have a safe return home; ending by the true Highland 'Nis! nis! nis! Sit air, a-nis! A-ris! a-ris! a-ris! (pronounced 'Neesh! neesh! neesh! Sheet eir, a-neesh! A rees! a rees! a rees!') which means, 'Now! now! now! That to him now! Again! again! again!' which was responded to by cheering from all. Grant then proposed 'three cheers for the Duke of Athole,' which was also very warmly responded to – my pony (good 'Inchrory'), which went admirably, rather resenting the vehemence of Brown's cheering.

After the steep and precipitous part the glen opens out to reveal a flat, bare, moorland watershed, 1,500ft (458m) at its highest point, with views to the Aberdeenshire mountains beyond. It was not the Bynack stream that the royal party crossed at the 'County March', but Dubh Alltan, where several centuries ago the men of Mar attempted to dig a trench through the level ground to divert this stream towards Deeside rather than Atholl. However, they were routed by the men of Atholl and its course remained unchanged. Here the party halted and a number of toasts were proposed and drunk. The Queen was moved by the traditional Gaelic salutation, as is shown by her attempts at pronunciation in her journal.

We then went on again for about three miles to the Bainoch, which we reached at ten minutes to six, when it was already nearly dark. As we approached the 'shiel,' the pipers struck up and played. The ponies went so well with the pipes, and altogether it was very pleasant to ride and walk with them. They played the 'Athole Highlanders' when we started, and again in coming in.

Lady Fife had very kindly come down to the Bainoch herself, where she gave us tea, which was very welcome.

Darkness was falling as the company reached Bynack Lodge, where Lady Fife was waiting to greet them with refreshing tea. The Queen and Albert bade farewell to the Duke, wishing him a safe journey home as it was such a dark night.

We then got into our carriages, wishing the Duke good-by. He was going back the whole way, which was certainly rather a hazardous proceeding – at least an adventurous one, considering the night, and that there was no moon – and what the road was! We got home safely at a quarter past eight. The night was quite warm, though slightly showery, but became very clear and starlight later.

> *We had travelled 69 miles to-day and 60 yesterday. This was the pleasantest and most enjoyable expedition I **ever** made, and the recollection of it will always be most agreeable to me, and increase my wish to do more! Was so glad dear Louis (who is a charming companion) was with us. Have enjoyed nothing as much, or indeed felt so much cheered by any thing since my great sorrow. Did not feel tired. We ladies did not dress, and dined en famille, looking at maps of the Highlands after dinner.*

The 'great sorrow' mentioned by the Queen in her diary was the death of her mother Victoria, Duchess of Kent. Such was the Queen's pleasure at spending a day in Atholl after such a lengthy interval, that she wrote to Duchess Anne on the day following her return to Balmoral:

My dearest Duchess

I cannot let a day pass without telling you how delighted we were with our beautiful ride back thro' Glen Tilt and we accomplished it safely including the difficult fording of the Tarff – my only anxiety is how the Duke got back. We went quite safely thro'. I can't say it would be a pleasant land to go at night . . .

It was such a picturesque journey. So wild in every way, and I can assure you that nothing has cheered me more in all my deep sorrow than these Highland Expeditions. . . . We got back here by a quarter past eight.

The Duke asked several questions about John Brown, my Highland servant yesterday. He has been at Balmoral in charge of the horses. But for the last three years he has been my personal servant here and always attends me when I go out – walking, riding and on all our travelling expeditions. He is an excellent, handy servant, able to do any thing. He always remains at Balmoral and is the son – one of 7 of a farmer here. He also is an invaluable, shrewd and trustworthy man.

This letter transmits the Queen's joy at being back in Atholl again, and also perhaps reveals her thoughts about John Brown. He was a farmer's son and was recommended for royal service by Dr Andrew Robertson, the Queen's Commissioner on Deeside in whose employment he had been previously. He is first mentioned in the Queen's diary on 11 September 1849. He was described as a rough, handsome, intelligent man with a strong arm, long legs, curly hair and beard, blue eyes and a firm chin. He knew every hill track and stream for miles around, and was invaluable on family excursions in always knowing which way to go and in setting out the picnic luncheons in a way that pleased the Queen. He quickly rose from being a humble servant and by 1851 was leading the Queen's pony. She obviously had further responsibilities in mind for him, as she recorded in her diary entry of 11 February 1865:

> *Have decided that Brown should remain permanently & make himself useful in other ways besides leading my pony as he is so very dependable.*

Henceforth he became her personal attendant and was known as 'The Queen's Highland Servant'.

Return to Blair Castle

Duchess Anne had already written to the Queen and her letter reveals some of the problems of travelling through a remote glen in the middle of a dark night.

Madam,

Your Majesty having been pleased to express a wish to hear how the Duke made out his return to Blair after escorting Your Majesty through Glen Tilt, I take an early opportunity of reporting his safe arrival here at 1 a.m. on Thursday morning. We trust that Your Majesty's drive to Balmoral proved successful likewise and that it has not been followed by much fatigue.

After Your Majesty's departure from the Baineach the Duke and his party started homewards and as it soon grew dark, each man tied a white pocket handkerchief to his back to guide the one immediately behind him – while Jock McAra took the lead as pilot. At the County March the whisky remaining in the Duke's flask was finished to drink Your Majesty's health. The darkness having increased, & the ground being precipitous, it was found advisable to light 4 policemen's lanterns with which they forded the Tarf 2+2, arm in arm, singing 'God save the Queen' and the Duke says the effect altogether with the falls and the light gleaming on it was beautiful.

They heard the harts roaring from the moment they left the Baineach and near Dal Chronachie Jock saw a deer on the path immediately in front before them which would scarcely get out of their way. At Dal Chronachie they found a bottle of Selzer Water, marking the spot where Your Majesty had rested; this proved very acceptable mixed with some sherry from Mr Sutton's flask; but each of the men had a taste of it plain which caused many wry faces, Jock remarking it was very like seawater. They reached Forest Lodge at ¼ past 10 having made the distance in exactly four hours. All walked back in high spirits not the least tired. The night was so dark that the Pipers did not play till within the last mile of Forest Lodge: but the Duke begs to inform Your Majesty that he ascertained in going that they both played through the Poll Tarf. The pony carriage had been left at the Lodge for driving down the glen but only proved a hindrance. The Duke and some of the party having got into it, proceeded safely till near the Marble Quarry Bridge but there, in the endeavor to keep away from the opposite and more dangerous edge, the carriage ran against a stone-faced bank – and only the united strength of 5 men got it back into the middle of the road, minus one splash board step.

Shortly after passing the Queen's Well one of the horses fell and broke his knees; the Duke and party then thought it advisable to get out and walk the remaining 4 miles which was probably just as well as after passing the Bridge of Coinleam the other horse jibbed going up the hill and proposed to stop there. The Duke and Mr Sutton were safe and sound and the former much the better for the experience which he is sure if more frequent, add to his life, and begs me to say that he hopes Your Majesty's future visits will not be at such long intervals.

It has given me so much pleasure to see Your Majesty and the Prince again at

Blair. I am glad that Princess Alice now knows the look of my house.
Your Majesty's ever faithful
and affectionate servant

A. Athole.

Queen Victoria replied to Duchess Anne on 18 October:

My dear Duchess,
Our letters crossed – and I thank you only now for your most amusing letter. We were
so glad that the Duke got back safe but it was very fortunate that the carriage incident
was no worse.

I write today to ask you to be so very kind as to tell me the name of the road we
drove on our way up Glen Tilt. I think I have forgotten; it was my favourite walk. We
set out so often . . . and like wise the name of the spot where the march was passed and
the Duke drank my health.

So have but three days more here and then we return to Windsor – it will be a
terrible trial there. . . .

These expeditions, when the Queen would set off with a few companions in a carriage
and on horseback to explore the countryside, were undoubtedly the highlights of her Scottish
travels. Sometimes she would be away from Balmoral for several days, staying in simple inns
in remote places and it gave her some sense of being an ordinary person, rather than the
sovereign of the most powerful country in the world. They were a stark contrast to her life of
ceremony at Windsor and the older she grew the more important they became to her. These
were the happiest days of the life and can justly be called her 'dream days'.

Within two months of this excursion Prince Albert died of what was diagnosed at the
time as typhoid fever, and the Queen never fully recovered from her tragic loss, though she
lived for another forty years. She had depended on him for everything and from that moment
on loneliness was always with her.

On 1 January 1862 Queen Victoria wrote to Duchess Anne, enclosing a locket in which
to keep the lock of Prince Albert's hair she had received earlier from the Queen at the time
of his death at Windsor. It was inside a tiny, black-edged envelope which was inscribed: 'The
precious Hair of my beloved & adored Husband, Dec. 14, 1861 for the dear D. of Atholl.'

Dearest Duchess,   *Osborne: Jan:1*
I send you with this the little Locket which **You** *are the* ***first*** *to receive and which I hope*
you will often wear. You should have a copy of the Inscription made for I fear it may
wear out; Anyrate I will write it out for you. **I** *think you* **have** *some dear Hair?*

You must ***ever*** *be* **most** *particularly dear to me having been with me thro' this*
time of **awful** *misery when My dear happy, happy Home has been for* **ever** *&* ***ever*** *des-*
troyed, & it must be a **great** *tie between us. I* **do** *trust in that Father in Heaven who*
gave me my happiness & who has taken it away but **I do** *feel that it* **is almost** *more*

*than I **can bear**! The agony I suffer I can't describe – & tho' I will not neglect what I was told to do for my health, & will struggle on in this weary pilgrimage of ours without my blessed precious adored Angel, you will **all** understand **I cannot** wish it should be for long! My beloved One is near me, near me, & loves me as **ever** and **then** I trust I **shall** be **fit** to join Him, & to be worthy of Him – **then never** to part! Oh! that blessed thought. It sustains me amidst my **utter** desolation, amidst moments when it seems as tho' the Heavens closed over me! . . .*

*But oh! it was a very different feeling to the ferment which overwhelmed me after my beloved Mother's death. I was **dreadfully** distressed & very shaken but oh! I had no feeling of **utter, utter** desolation – **I** had my precious One by me to support & comfort & cheer me between my bursts of sorrow – And now?*

I am

Yours affly

The Queen probably felt able to unleash these very private feelings to the Duchess as she had been in waiting at Windsor at the time of the Prince's death, and had been a strong support to her.

Now the Queen sought solace in the places she knew, especially those with a deep and fond association with the Prince. The coming of the railway made the journey to Balmoral quicker, simpler and more comfortable and she began to visit Scotland twice a year, making a short stay in the early summer, followed by a much longer one in the autumn.

CHAPTER FOUR

1863
An Errand of Mercy

BLAIR CASTLE,
TUESDAY 15 SEPTEMBER

When Queen Victoria learned that the 6th Duke was terminally ill, she decided to break her train journey from Windsor to Balmoral at Perth and pay him a visit. Lady Augusta Bruce, formerly Lady in Waiting to the Queen's late mother the Duchess of Kent and who became engaged later that year to Arthur Stanley, Dean of Westminster, wrote to Duchess Anne on 11 September to outline their plans:

Beloved Duchess,

. . . I write this line in haste to say that the Queen has set Her heart on going to see you and the dear Duke on Tuesday. Nobody is to know it, but while the Royal Children rest, H M would run up in a Special Train to Blair & back again only to show you even more if possible Her deep sympathy & unless it was bad for him she would wish to do it and would not wish him to get up but just to let Her see him a moment in bed if that is most convenient.

H M says you were with Her in Her trial and Blair was the last place she visited with the Prince so to Her it would be most congenial to be allowed to do this & besides She feels now a right to be there when there's sorrow & suffering. H M would change Her dress & come on directly & return after ½ an hour's time or so by the special to Perth.

*If it really will not **harm him or you** let Her do it, you would send a plain carriage and have no preparation . . .*

Yrs vy affly

Augusta Bruce

First proposals to build a main railway line from Perth to Inverness following a direct route through the Grampian Mountains were put forward in 1845, but the Parliamentary Bill for this scheme was thrown out as it was considered impossible for steam locomotives to haul trains over Drumochter Summit. Eventually the line was opened on 9 September 1863 and only six days later Queen Victoria travelled on it by special train to Blair Atholl.

Accompanying the Queen were General Grey, Lady Augusta Bruce and Princess Helena, Lenchen, the Queen's third daughter, born in 1846. She was to marry Prince Christian of Schleswig-Holstein in 1865.

The Queen's diary takes up the story:

> *Balmoral, Tuesday, September 15, 1863.*
> *At twenty minutes to eight we reached Perth, where we breakfasted and dressed, and at twenty minutes past nine I left with Lenchen, Augusta Bruce and General Grey for Blair, going past Dunkeld, where we had not been since 1844, and which is so beautifully situated, and Pitlochry, through the splendid Pass of Killiecrankie (which we so often drove through in 1844) past Mr Butter's place Faskally, on to Blair, having a distant peep at the entrance to Glen Tilt, and Schiehallion, which it made and makes me sick to think of. At the small station were a few people – the poor Duke's Highlanders (keepers), the dear Duchess, Lord Tullibardine, and Captain Drummond of Megginch.*
>
> *The Duchess was much affected, still more so when she got in the carriage with me. Lenchen and the others went in the boat carriage, the one **we** had gone in not two years ago!*

At Blair Atholl station a guard of honour of Atholl Highlanders, many of whom had accompanied the Queen through Glen Tilt when she and Prince Albert passed through on their way to Balmoral two years earlier, were now on parade on the platform. They were commanded by Lord Tullibardine, heir to the 6th Duke and Captain John Drummond, who had been in charge of the Guard at Dunkeld Bridge in 1842. The royal train arrived at Blair 'punctual to the minute' and the Queen's coach stopped opposite a length of cloth in the Murray tartan which stretched across the platform to the waiting carriage, where Duchess Annes was ready to greet the Queen. Because of the sadness of the occasion, there was no cheering from the crowd of about 200 people who had gathered outside the station as the royal party set off for the castle, escorted by the Highlanders.

Blair Castle

> *We drove at once to the house which we had visited in such joyful and high spirits October 9, two years ago. The Duchess took me to the same room which I had been in that day, and after talking a little to me of this dreadful affliction she went to see if the Duke was ready. She soon returned, and I followed her downstairs along the passage full of stags' horns which we walked along, together with the poor Duke, in 1861. When I went in, I found him standing up very much altered; it was very sad. He kissed my hand, gave me the white rose which, according to tradition, is presented by the Lords of Athole on the occasion of the Sovereign's visit, and we sat*

Lord Tullibardine, later the 7th Duke

a little while with him. It is a small room, full of his rifles and other implements and attributes of sport – now for ever useless to him! A sad, sad contrast. He seemed very much pleased and gratified.

Coming quite soon after the death of Prince Albert, Queen Victoria was very distressed when she saw how ill her dear friend the Duke of Atholl really was – he had been suffering for several months. The previous day Miss Amelia MacGregor had picked a white rose in the garden, which the Duke gave to his Queen on her arrival at the castle. This really should have been a red rose, as a charter of the Earldom of Atholl granted by King James III on 18 March 1481 stipulated a yearly payment of a red rose at the Feast of the Nativity of St John the Baptist. From this sprang the tradition that a red rose should always be presented to a visiting monarch.

We went upstairs again and took some breakfast, in the very same room where we breakfasted on that very happy, never-to-be-forgotten day, full of joy and expectation. While we were breakfasting, the door opened, and in walked the Duke in a thick MacDougal. Mrs Drummond and Miss Moncreiffe (the Duchess's pretty, amiable future daughter-in-law) were there, and also Miss MacGregor, but we did not see her.

This was the Queen's first meeting with Louisa Moncreiffe, eldest daughter of Sir Thomas Moncreiffe. A few weeks later she and Lord Tullibardine were married, becoming the 7th Duke and Duchess the following January and she was very much a society beauty of her time.

> *The poor Duke insisted on going with me to the station, and he went in the carriage with the Duchess and me. At the station he got out, walked about, and gave directions. I embraced the dear Duchess and gave the Duke my hand, saying, 'Dear duke, God bless you!' He had asked permission that his men, the same who had gone through the glen on that happy day two years ago, might give me a cheer, and he led them on himself. Oh! it was so dreadfully sad! To think of the contrast to the time two years ago, when my darling was so well and I so happy with him, and just beginning to recover from my great sorrow for dearest Mama's death – looking forward to many more such delightful expeditions; and the poor Duke then full of health and strength, walking the whole way, and at the 'March' stopping to drink our health and asking us to come again whenever we liked, and giving a regular Highland cheer in Highland fashion, returned by our men, the pipers playing, and all, so gay, so bright! And I so eager for next year's expeditions, which I ought not to have been! Oh! how little we know what is before us! How uncertain is life! I felt very sad, but was so much occupied with the poor Duke for whom I truly grieved that I did not feel the trial of returning to Blair in such terribly altered circumstances, as I should otherwise have done.*

The Queen stayed for an hour at the castle, and there was much surprise that the Duke was able to escort her back to the station, as he was then so ill. At the station the Queen spoke to Mr T. C. Bruce, chairman of the Perth and Inverness Railway Company, whose brother was Governor of India, and expressed her satisfaction with the new line and the pleasure it gave her to pass through such magnificent scenery. The Hon Mr Bruce travelled with the engine driver in the cab for the journeys from and to Perth while, in case of breakdown, the general manager of the company travelled in the train along with several engineers and the secretary of the Perth and Dunkeld Railway Company.

> *At Stanley Junction we joined the others, and proceeded as usual to Aboyne, whence we drove in open carriages – Lenchen, Alfred, and Baby with me – and reached Balmoral at twenty minutes past six. It was very cold. Bertie and Alix were at the door, and stayed a little while afterwards. How strange they should be at Abergeldie! A few years ago dear Mama used to receive us.*

Two of the Queen's children were waiting for her in the Royal Train at Stanley Junction, from which she continued her journey to Balmoral. Prince Alfred, Affie, was her second son, born in 1844, who became the Duke of Edinburgh and Saxe-Coburg. Princess Beatrice, affectionately known as 'Baby', was the ninth and youngest child, born in 1857, and perhaps it was she who inspired the present Duke and Duchess of York to name their first daughter Beatrice.

Princess Beatrice in 1863

Victoria's eldest son, Prince Albert Edward, Bertie, then Prince of Wales, with his wife, Princess Alexandra, was waiting for them when they arrived at Balmoral. Their Deeside residence was within two miles of Balmoral at Abergeldie Castle, a massive and imposing castle with a turreted square block house and an estate extending for ten miles along the River Dee.

As soon as she arrived at Balmoral, Queen Victoria wrote to Duchess Anne to express her great sorrow:

> *My Dearest Duchess,*   *Balmoral, Sept:15. 1863.*
> *I cannot go to rest tonight without trying to say **again all** I feel for you & for His grace, the terribly suffering dear Invalid! **Deep,** most deep is my sympathy & I wish it were in **my** power to do anything to cheer or comfort you both. I wish you would tell me if there is **any** thing I could do to gratify or please the Duke, any wish for any thing which would please him. I would willingly have gone much further to visit him & am truly thankful I was able to go today. But it was a **very** sad visit! You must I think still have my letter to you after our last visit Oct 9-61 – in which I told you **how** I enjoyed that visit, & that I longed to repeat it – & that its wild & picturesque character had done me real good & been that thing which had cheered me since dear Mama's loss! And the Duke*

*was so well – my **Own** Darling was so well & the Duke drank our healths & said he*
hoped we would come again whenever we liked! . . .
Ever yrs affly
& sadly

Princess Victoria, now the Crown Princess of Prussia, was away at the time and, saddened at not having a first-hand account of the visit to Blair Castle and of the Duke's health, wrote to Duchess Anne from Abergeldie on 7 October 1863:

I was so sorry not to have been here when the Queen paid you a visit at Blair and to
hear so sad an account of the Duke's health.

I hope you will not think it in any way indiscreet but I could not resist writing
to enquire about the Duke. He always was so very kind to me when a child, and I cannot
describe how sorry I am to hear of his sad state of health – and how I feel for you dear
Duchess.

This is my 1st visit to the dear Highlands since all the sad changes that have taken
place – Balmoral without dear Papa – seems too strange and sad – and that House
without Grandmama – all is so altered to us – and the dear place is so unchanged!

Please remember me to the Duke and say all that is kind. Please tell him that I
recollect Blair as well as possible – the house, the terrace and the grounds – also the falls
of the Bruar, where I drove in a little carriage with your son. Goodbye dear Duchess, the
Prince wishes to be remembered to you.

George, 6th Duke of Atholl, died on 16 January 1864 and was buried in St Bride's churchyard in Old Blair. His beloved Atholl Highlanders were with him to the very end, carrying the coffin shoulder high in relays to the church – and firing a farewell salute of 49 guns, to represent his age.

Just before the Duke's death Princess Victoria paid an informal call to Blair Castle and in her letter of 17 February 1865 to Duchess Anne recalled this visit:

Never shall I forget that sad visit to your lovely Blair – which is one of my earliest
recollections and the last time I saw the Duke, I felt remorse at that time and how deeply
it affected me to see him so – and to go away feeling that I should never see him again.

The Duke had always been so kind to me from a little child and I well know the
Queen valued the attachment of one of the most loyal of her Highland subjects.

Queen Victoria was told of the Duke of Atholl's death on the day he died and immediately wrote to the Duchess:

*My **own** dearest Duchess,*   *Osborne Jan:16.1864*
*A **broken** hearted widow writes to **one** who **now** belongs to that **saddest** of sisterhoods.*
*Oh! could I but fold you in my arms as you did **me** on **that dreadful** Night!*
Words are poor and weak to say what I feel for you! Your dear beautiful Letters

of the 9th & 10th reached me on the 12th & I cannot sufficiently Thank you for it –
and for letting **me** *know* **your** *inmost thoughts. I earnestly trust that the End has been*
peaceful & painless & that you can dwell with comfort on your dear Husband's release
& happiness **now***. But* **how** *your loving devoted heart will feel the blank after these*
months of weary, anxious watching! It is so awful – the contrast of utter silence – and
of the utter impossibility of doing any thing any more for the dear object of one's work
. . .

Duchess Anne's bond with the Queen was strengthened even more now that both were
widows and her relationship with the Queen's children flowered and cut straight across the
generations.

THE QUEEN'S VISIT TO THE DUKE OF ATHOLE
15th SEPTEMBER 1863

Let Athole's hills the story tell;
And every Highland Stream,
In ever-flowing numbers, swell
The music of the theme:—
The beauty, and the lovingness,
The kindness of the scene;
The goodness and the charity,
Of Britain's gracious Queen!
For never has a woman's love
More touchingly been seen;
And never yet has pity shone
With brighter, holier beam,
Than when, by Tay's fair flowing tide,
The Monarch turned her steps aside,
Regardless of the toil to come
Ere yet she reach her Highland home:
Thoughtless of all, except the deep
Deep grief in Athole's tower:
Wondering if sympathy might steep
That sorrow for one hour;
If words of hers might bring relief,
Might mitigate so great a grief;
Or look of hers have power to bless
Her servants, in their sore distress.

CHAPTER FIVE

1865
First Visit to the 'Cottage'

DUNKELD,
MONDAY 9–FRIDAY 13 OCTOBER

Queen Victoria's thoughts kept returning to the peace and calm of the 'Cottage' beside the Tay in Dunkeld that she had first seen in 1844 and plans were made for a visit in the autumn. The date of 9 October was confirmed in a letter Princess Helena wrote to the Dowager Duchess Anne on 16 September 1865:

Dearest Duchess,

She desires me now to tell you that the 9th October would be about the day she would propose leaving here for Dunkeld or the 10th if the weather were bad on the preceding day and she would remain 2 or 3 nights according as it is possible and hopes that would not be too long. She also desires me to ask you that her visit might be kept quite a secret or else people might come to Dunkeld and that would spoil all the pleasure of the visit.

If you knew how I am looking forward to going with dear Mama, it will be such a pleasure to see you again.

Yours affectionately,

Helena

Once again the Queen hoped for as private a visit as possible, though several newspapers, including the *Perthshire Advertiser* and the *Constitutional & Perthshire Agricultural & General Advertiser* covered the visit. The Queen would have preferred an earlier date, as is shown in her letter of 21 September 1865:

Tho' Helena wrote to you to propose Monday 9th or Tuesday 10th, I was thinking about the availability of an earlier day as the weather and the days might be getting bad. I would therefore prefer Monday or Tuesday 2nd or 3rd for 3 nights. If the weather was very bad I might delay it for a day or 2.

Helena will come with me and a Lady who would be lodged at the inn – one of my keepers of the Wardrobe would come with her and help in dressing Helena. Brown I would also wish to have in the house.

St Adamnan's: 'the Duchess's nice, snug little cottage . . .' – Queen Victoria

This preferred date was not possible and Princess Helena replied on 26 September to say that:

Mama desires me to thank you for your letter and to tell you that she would come to Dunkeld on the 9th as that will suit you. She is sorry you cannot receive her over the 2nd or 3rd but quite understands your reasons. We trust the weather will remain as glorious as it is now for our expedition.

Meanwhile, General Grey was busy making all the arrangements for the journey and was content to follow the route suggested by Duchess Anne. This proposed travelling by carriage through the Spittal of Glenshee and Kirkmichael to Pitcarmick in Strathardle and then riding over the hill to Dunkeld. On 2 October he wrote to Duchess Anne telling her she was:

. . . quite at liberty to speak in confidence to Mr Keir (Kindrogan) & arrange every thing with him for Monday next – this day week. The wind with us is far round to the East & the sky is overcast. I hope we are not to have a change of weather.

Once again Princess Helena was to accompany the Queen along with her Lady in Waiting, Lady Jane Ely, John Brown and General Grey who was to meet them at Pitcarmick. Queen Victoria's diary takes up the journey:

Princess Beatrice in 1864, who was left at Balmoral with Prince Arthur

Monday, October 9, 1865.
A thick, misty, very threatening morning! There was no help for it, but it was sadly
provoking. It was the same once or twice in former happy days, and my dear Albert
always said we could not alter it, but must leave it as it was, and make the best of
it. Our three little ones breakfasted with me. I was grieved to leave my precious Baby
and poor Leopold behind. At ten started with Lenchen and Janie Ely (the same
attendants on the box). General Grey had gone on an hour and a half before.

'Baby' Beatrice was eight years old at this time and Prince Leopold, the Queen's fourth
son, was twelve. He was a very delicate child and suffered from haemophilia, about which very
little was known in those days. Despite this he was a high-spirited boy, who later developed a
keen interest in politics and was created Duke of Albany in 1882.

We took post-horses at Castleton. It rained more or less the whole time. Then came
the long well-known stage to the Spital of Glenshee, which seemed to me longer than
ever. The mist hung very thick over the hills. We changed horses there, and about a
quarter of an hour after we had left it, we stopped to lunch in the carriage. After
some delay we went on and turned into Strathardle, and then, leaving the
Blairgowrie road, down to the farm of Pitcarmich, shortly before coming to which
Mr Small Keir of Kindrogan met us and rode before us to this farm. Here we found

Mr Patrick Small Keir of Kindrogan

General Grey and our ponies, and here the dear Duchess of Athole and Miss MacGregor met us, and we got out and went for a short while into the farmhouse, where we took some wine and biscuit.

Strathardle

Pitcarmick was part of the 10,000-acre Kindrogan estate owned by Mr Patrick Small Keir, whose father had been presented to the Queen in Dunkeld in 1842 and had helped to guard her at Blair Castle in 1844. Patrick took over the estate on the death of his father in 1860 and at the time of the Queen's visit was a captain in the Atholl Highlanders. Pitcarmick possessed an extensive area of hill grazing for sheep and the dwelling house stood on a little knoll beside a burn and was home for the farm grieve, Peter Forbes, described as, 'a capital carpenter, made all his own furniture and could turn his hand to any useful aim'.

That particular morning, Mrs Forbes could have been seen tending two flocks of 'beautifully white turkies and equally spotless geese', while her two daughters were inside preparing for the royal visit. The elder was a school teacher in Blair Atholl, suffering on the day in question from acute toothache. That morning they had all set to work vigorously to get the place ready for the Queen.

Miss Amelia Murray MacGregor kept a journal recording this visit to Dunkeld, and vividly describes the everyday happenings during the Queen's three-day stay:

Miss Amelia MacGregor, who diligently recorded every detail of the Queen's 1865 visit

*The ladies amidst their busy avocations discovered that whenever they ran downstairs and into the next house to fetch something, their wet feet brought muddy steps to dirty the stair, so when all their preparations were completed, the staircase was cleaned and they resolved to avoid going out again if possible. Soon afterwards the shrill sound of 'cheep, cheep, cheep', was heard with a resounding 'schu, schu, schu' from Miss Keir. This was an invasion of young chickens who made sure that **their** presence would be acceptable and wished to force their way upstairs! Their dirty little foot-prints were very distressing to the inner garrison, but by a combined effort, they were discomfited and forced to retreat to the door where the hollow of an old millstone formed a comfortable basin for their small beaks to sup the rain.*

At twelve noon Mr Patrick Small Keir arrived from Kindrogan with his daughter Catherine, his niece Frances, the daughter of Captain Murray of Croftinloan, and Duchess Anne. Miss MacGregor records their arrival:

At noon Mr Keir's carriage drove down the narrow road with its several turnings, and through the small archway formed unintentionally, between the range of barns and stables on either side, with a wooden trough overhead, conveying water from the Burn to the Thrashing Mill. Just room to alight at the foot of the grassy knowe pertaining to the house, and the carriage turned away to the stables, whilst its inmates walked up the slope and entered the first Dwelling.

The Queen on Fyvie, with John Brown (left) and John Grant in 1865

At one o'clock General Grey arrived and he was permitted to eat his lunch 'very tidily without disturbing the order of the Table'. Afterwards he went outside and chatted to Peter Forbes, who described him as 'an uncommonly sensible man'. Meanwhile the ladies 'now took the rough pieces remaining after trimming the chickens, to the Bothy and there sitting on the blue kists, they ate their luncheon on principle tho' too anxious and excited to care much about it'.

Queen Victoria changed horses at the Spittal of Glenshee and, after a brief stop beside the road, arrived at Pitcarmick in a carriage drawn by four magnificent greys just before three o'clock, amid great excitement. The royal party went indoors to a small room where a fire was blazing and tartan plaids covered the floor. A cloth was laid on the table and cold chicken was cut up and arranged artistically with several bottles of wine and seltzer water. A small room nearby was set up as a dressing room and, having no window, was lit by a candle. Because the Queen and Princess had already eaten they were unable to do justice to the feast spread before them and instead drank only a little wine and seltzer water, ate some biscuits and did not linger long.

> *Then we mounted our ponies (I on dear Fyvie, Lenchen on Brechin), and started our course across the hill. There was much mist. This obscured the view, which otherwise would have been very fine. At first there was a rough road, but soon there was nothing but a sheep-track, and hardly that, through heather and stones up a pretty steep hill. Mr Keir could not keep up with the immense pace of Brown and Fyvie, which distanced everyone; so he had to drop behind, and his keeper acted as guide. There was by this time heavy driving rain, with a thick mist.*

The Queen was mounted on her favourite pony, Fyvie, led by John Brown, while Helena rode Brechin, often ridden in former times by Prince Albert and led on this occasion by Morgan, a tall, dark Balmoral Highlander. General Grey and Lady Ely, with Duchess Anne on her grey pony Grouse and Amelia MacGregor on a piebald called Cantharella, followed behind. The men forming the escort included John Grant, head stalker at Balmoral, a ghillie named Kennedy who attended Lady Ely and Donald Stewart, one of the Queen's ghillies, who carried the food. Duchess Anne had one of her men, Alexander Matthews, leading postillion, while there were four from Kindrogan: Donald MacFarlane, keeper; Alex Seaton, under keeper; Donald Robertson, shepherd and Charlie Fergusson, under gardener.

The cavalcade left Pitcarmick just before four o'clock in the pouring rain, with Mr Small Keir leading the way on foot. They followed a peat road beside the Pitcarmick Burn and eventually this degenerated into a rough sheep-track, which Mr Keir had attempted to improve a few days previously by removing the rough rocks and boulders that were in the way.

> *About a little more than an hour took us to the 'March', where two of the Dunkeld men met us, John MacGregor, the Duke's head wood-forester, and Gregor MacGregor, the Duchess's gamekeeper; and the former acted as guide. The Duchess and Miss MacGregor were riding with us. We went from here through larch woods, the rain pouring at times violently. We passed (after crossing the Dunkeld March) Little Loch Oishne, and Loch Oishne, before coming to Loch Ordie. Here dripping wet we arrived at about a quarter-past six, having left Pitcarmick at twenty minutes to four. It was dark already from the very bad weather. We went into a lodge here, and had tea and whisky, and Lenchen had to get herself dried, as she was so wet.*

Dunkeld March

John Brown was a very fast walker and Mr Small Keir found it impossible to keep in front. The track climbs to a height of 1,500ft (458m), where the boundary with Dunkeld is marked by a solid stone dyke and here, at the 'Queen's Gate', stood 'Little' Gregor MacGregor, 'a very promising specimen of the Clan, aged 16 and already considered a keeper' and John MacGregor, head forester on the Atholl Estate, 'whose bearing and manly appearance the

Loch Ordie Lodge and a party from the Perth Nature Association in 1883

Queen was pleased to observe, recognizing in him, the independent pride of a Highlander of his race'. He was a celebrated piper who had played for the Queen at Taymouth Castle in 1842. His grandfather, also John, had been a man, 'far famed in his day, for his profiency in the martial music of the Highlands and not less for his personal agility and warlike spirit'. He had supported the Jacobite cause, and joined the army as a piper on its march to Dunkeld in 1745.

At the march the royal party entered the Loch Oishne plantation, which covered over 2,000 acres with larch trees planted by the 4th Duke in 1825–26. Forty years later many of the trees had died, with others destroyed by forest fires, so that the remaining trees were thinly scattered and interspersed with heather. This area was never replanted and is now a wild expanse of heather, bracken and rocks, with a few larch trees surviving on exposed knolls.

The rain-drenched cavalcade continued along the path through the trees and passed Lochan Oisinneach Beag, a small pear-shaped loch and then, a little further on, Lochan Oisinneach Mor, from which point the track improved considerably.

Just after six o'clock they reached the shores of Loch Ordie, in the centre of another large plantation dating from 1815–16, which again was mainly larch with a few oaks. Loch Ordie lies at an altitude of 1,000ft (305m) in an amphitheatre of hills, and after another half mile they reached Loch Ordie Lodge, surrounded by trees on the southern bank of the loch. This was a shooting and fishing lodge which had been extended by Duchess Anne and part of it was home to one of her shepherds, William McCall. Here the party, no doubt thankfully, dismounted and drank some tea, hastily brewed by Miss MacGregor. Princess Helena was soaked to the skin and was taken into the kitchen to dry out in front of the peat fire. On being introduced, the Princess said, 'I am the Queen's daughter,' at which Mrs McCall exclaimed 'Ah. Indeed!' and warmly clasped her hand.

Lost in the Hills

About seven we drove off from Loch Ordie. There was no outrider, so we sent on first the other carriage with Lenchen, Lady Ely, and Miss MacGregor, and General Grey on the box, and I went with the Duchess in a phaeton which had a hood – Brown and Grant going behind. It was pitch-dark, and we had to go through a wood, and I must own I was somewhat nervous.

At seven o'clock the party moved off on the carriage road from Loch Ordie. The Queen and Duchess Anne were in a pony phaeton, with John Brown and John Grant on the box behind, drawn by two horses, Eclipse and Life, driven by Robert Bowles, one of the Dunkeld postillions. Princess Helena, Lady Ely and Miss MacGregor, with General Grey on the box, set off in a sociable, an open four-wheeled carriage, so Miss MacGregor sat next to the Princess, holding up an umbrella in an attempt to protect her from the rain, which was still falling incessantly. It had been arranged that Patrick Small Keir would stay in Dunkeld as his duties were completed and he travelled a more direct way with John MacGregor along a grassy drive cut into the side of the hill, with trees on one side and a steep and wooded bank on the other. This was a stiff pull for horses going up to Loch Ordie, so a more circuitous route, with easier gradients, via Lochs Rotmell and Dowally, was often used. Despite the fact that Smith, the coachman, had previously driven down the grassy drive at night, he was nervous of the route and 'begged leave to go down by the lower and less customary road, considering it the safest'. The Duchess, thinking he should know best, agreed somewhat reluctantly. By this time the night was pitch dark and it was still raining in torrents.

We had not gone very far when we perceived that we were on a very rough road, and I became much alarmed, though I would say nothing. A branch took off Grant's cap, and we had to stop for Brown to go back and look for it with one of the carriage lamps. This stoppage was most fortunate, for he then discovered we were on a completely wrong road. Grant and Brown had both been saying, 'This is no carriage-road; it is full of holes and stones.' Miss MacGregor came to us in great distress, saying she did not know what to do, for that coachman, blinded by the driving rain, had mistaken the road, and that we were in a track for carting wood. What was to be done, no one at this moment seemed to know – whether to try and turn the carriage (which proved impossible) or to take a horse out and send the postilion back to Loch Ordie to get assistance. At length we heard from General Grey that we could go on, though where we should get out, no one could exactly tell. Grant took a lamp out of the carriage and walked before the horses, while Brown led them; and this reassured me. But the road was very rough, and we had to go through some deep holes full of water. At length, in about twenty minutes, we saw a light and passed a lodge, where we stopped and inquired where we were, for we had already come upon a good road. Our relief was great when we were told we were all right. Grant and Brown got up behind, and we trotted along the high road fast enough. Just before we came to the lodge, General Grey called out to ask which way the Duchess thought we should go, and Brown answered in her name, 'The Duchess don't know at all where we are,' as it was so dark she could not recognise familiar places.

After driving a short way along a reasonable track, the Duchess became aware that the road surface had deteriorated and this surprised her, as it had only recently been repaired and improved. However, it was not until John Grant's cap was swept off by a branch that they fully realised that something was wrong. When Grant and Brown went in search of the missing piece of headgear they saw the bad state of the road and chorused, 'not fit for any carriages'. The coachman confided to Miss MacGregor that because of the driving rain he had missed the turning and, worse still, had no idea where they were. He and General Grey set off with the carriage lamps to reconnoitre, and Amelia MacGregor records the whole episode succintly in her journal:

*. . . Here in the thick of a vast wood, the Queen of Great Britain was detained under a pouring rain. A high bank clothed with trees rose on one side of the carriage, on the other there was a steep declivity; impossible for the carriage to turn, and yet it might be dangerous to proceed, lest an overturn should result. General Grey and the Queen's two Highlanders naturally knew nothing of the country, the Coachman and Postillion had the horses to look after, the Duchess had no man free to send back for assistance, and no one knew exactly where the party was. Was **this** the result of such carefully laid plans, such anxious preparations! – to go and mislead Our beloved Sovereign in a Wood, and keep her waiting in the rain. How very different all would have been had the poor Duke been alive, with his genius for organization and oh! how People would scoff and say Women were indeed little fit to manage things! Thoughts like these rushed through the minds of the Duchess and Miss MacGregor, although they strove rather to seek energetically for a remedy than to indulge in vain regrets. The Queen smoothed over the difficulty as much as possible; perfectly calm and cheerful Her Majesty expressed Her willingness either to get out and let an attempt be made to turn the carriage or to sit still and wait; the trying circumstances did not the least disturb Her Majesty's equanimity.*

General Grey returned shortly to report that, since only a short part of the bad road remained, it was possible to proceed with care and they would soon emerge on to a good road. On returning to the sociable, poor Amelia MacGregor fell knee deep in a pothole of water. Then all set off, with John Grant in front of the Queen's carriage and John Brown leading one of the horses. After great exertions and very careful driving both carriages negotiated the rough

'The Garry is very fine, rolling along over large stones . . . with birch and mountain ash growing down to the water's edge' – Queen Victoria

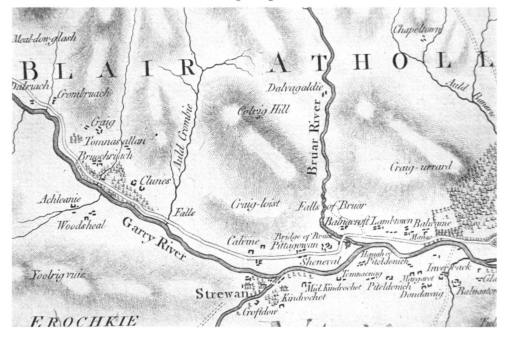

Queen Victoria's route to Blair Castle in 1861 is clearly shown on this 1783 map, following the north bank of the River Garry

'. . . Glen Tilt, which is most striking, the road winding along first on one side of the Tilt, and then on the other' – Queen Victoria (1861)

Many of the twelve men who escorted the Queen through Glen Tilt appear in this 1868 group of Atholl Hillmen: Donald MacBeath is on the far left, Jock McAra is third left and Sandy McAra is on the extreme right

Henry George Sutton with his deerhound Spey, who accompanied the 6th Duke to Bynack Lodge and on the eventful return journey in the dark to Blair Castle in 1861

Donald MacBeath as a sergeant major in full Atholl Highlander dress uniform in 1893

track, which was merely a forest road for extracting timber, and came out on the Upper Tulliemet road. From here they passed Countlich Lodge, probably where the Queen saw a light, and by way of a steep descent reached the main road between Guay and Kindallachan. Thence it was an easy four-mile trot to Dunkeld. Miss MacGregor suggested that the forest track, since it had been opened by the Queen in person, should henceforth be christened 'The Queen's Drive'.

Arrival at Dunkeld

At length at a quarter to nine we arrived quite safely at Dunkeld, at the Duchess's nice, snug little cottage, which is just outside the town, surrounded by fine large grounds. Two servants in kilts, and the steward, received us at the door. You come at once on the middle landing of the staircase, the cottage being built on sloping ground. The Duchess took me to my room, a nice little room, next to which was one for my wardrobe maid, Mary Andrews. Lenchen was upstairs near Miss MacGregor on one side of the drawing-room, which was given up to me as my sitting-room, and the Duchess's room on the other. Brown, the only other servant in the house below, Grant in the adjoining buildings to the house. The General and Lady Ely were at the hotel. We dined at half past nine in a small dining-room below, only Lenchen, the Duchess, Miss MacGregor and I. Everything so nice and quiet. The Duchess and Miss MacGregor carving, her three servants waiting. they were so kind, and we talked over the day's adventures. Lenchen and every one, except the Duchess and myself had been drenched. The Duchess and her cousin stayed a short while. Strange to say, it was four years to-day that we paid our visit to Blair and rode up Glen Tilt. How different!

The party arrived at last in Dunkeld just before nine o'clock, very wet and tired and exactly four years to the day since the Queen's favourite expedition through Glen Garry, stopping at Blair Castle for coffee and home to Balmoral by the memorable ride through Glen Tilt.

St Adamnan's Cottage was Duchess Anne's main residence and the Queen had first visited it briefly at the end of her three-week stay at Blair in 1844. It was a fairly large, double bow-fronted house, built in the latter part of the eighteenth century in front of the cathedral, overlooking the River Tay. Formerly it had been an inn, but in 1811 was much altered and modified to convert it into a private house. In 1828 the 4th Duke decided to pull down Dunkeld House, his main residence in the town and thereafter St Adamnan's became an occasional residence for the Atholl family. Although quite a large house by general standards, it was described in 1828 as being 'tho' beautiful in itself, must be confined in every room' and must indeed have seemed very restricted after the immense rooms of the old Dunkeld House. In 1900 the house was in such a bad state of repair, needing a large sum of money to restore it, that it was demolished, as plans were already well in hand to build a new house at Dunkeld, now the Dunkeld House Hotel.

The Queen's bedroom was near the conservatory and Mary Andrews, her wardrobe

James Mackie, Dunkeld gardener

maid, who left her service the following year, was next door. Princess Helena slept in the 'middle room', a small apartment at the top of the stairs beside Amelia MacGregor's room. Lady Ely and General Grey stayed at the Duke of Atholl's Arms in the town, there being no room for them at the 'Cottage'. James Mackie, the gardener, and Gregor MacGregor, the sixteen-year-old keeper, kept guard during the night, occasionally walking round the grounds in order to deter any intruders.

It is incredible for us now to reflect that the Queen of the most powerful country in the world had been completely lost, with only a few servants in attendance, in the woods among the mountains beyond Dunkeld on a cold, dark and wet October night for some hours with no-one having any knowledge of her whereabouts. Miss MacGregor records in her journal that over dinner 'the misadventure of the Woods formed the theme of very lively discourse', while the Queen's diary entry of 'Everything so nice and quiet' underlines the pleasure she felt at getting away from the pomp and ceremony of court to a house with the minimum of fuss.

St Colme's

Tuesday, October 10.
A hopelessly wet morning. I had slept well, but felt sad on awakening. Breakfasted alone with Lenchen downstairs, each day waited on by Brown. A dreadful morning,

pouring rain. Sat upstairs in the drawing-room, and wrote a good deal, being perfectly quiet and undisturbed.

Lenchen and I lunched with the Duchess and Miss MacGregor, and at four we drove up to the Duchess's very fine model farm of St Colme's, about four miles from Dunkeld; the Duchess and I in the phaeton, Lenchen, Janie Ely and Miss MacGregor going in the other carriage. We went all over the farm in detail, which is very like ours at Osborne and Windsor, much having been adopted from our farms there; and my dearest Husband had given the Duchess so much advice about it, that we both felt so sad he should not see it.

It was not until well into the afternoon that Queen Victoria ventured forth and drove with the other ladies four miles north to St Colme's, high up on the hillside on the east bank of the Tay. Up until the eighteenth century it had been called Rotmell, when it was renamed St Colme's, reverting again to its original name at the end of the last century. The Barony of Rotmell was acquired by the 1st Duke of Atholl in 1714 from a Henry Balneavis, in an exchange for the lands of Edradour.

St Colme's was the 'model' farm of the Dunkeld portion of the Atholl Estate, built just after 1800. It was an extensive, whitewashed, four-square complex of substantial buildings and steadings comprising stables, barns, byres, a smithy, a joiner's workshop and sheds from which turnips were conveyed in wagons along light rails. There was a threshing mill and saw mill, powered by a huge iron water wheel. An indication of the size and interior of the wing reserved for the Atholl family comes from a letter written by Mr Thomas Palliser, the factor, to the Duke on 7 June 1807:

. . . I have sent your Grace a plan of the two Rooms at St Columbes Farm to regulate the quantity and size of the Furniture. I think a Dozen chairs for each room, two small tables for the Drawing Room, a Dining Table with two round ends to answer as a Breakfast Table, or to make an addition to the Dining Table would be sufficient . . .

The situation of St Colme's was vividly described in 'The Highland Tay' at the turn of the century:

On the brow of the valley there is an open glade among the larch woods, from which gleams a series of low, white buildings, systematically arranged in a square. It looks like a mediaeval castle, or a barracks, and one is surprised to be told that it is the Duchess of Atholl's model farm. The uniformity of the architecture harmonises with the monotony of the surroundings to which it gives an imposing appearance.

On arriving at the farm, the Queen went into the wing at the south-east corner which was reserved for the Duchess's personal use, and they then made a tour of the extensive steadings with James Gillespie, the farm grieve. The Queen showed great interest in the smith and his assistant fashioning horseshoes and then went into Gillespie's house to meet his wife, three daughters and the youngest, a boy, whom the Queen thought a fine child for his age.

> *We took tea in the farmhouse, where the Duchess has kept one side quite for herself, and where she intends to live sometimes with Miss MacGregor, and almost by themselves. From here we drove back and stopped at the 'Byres', close by the stables, which were lit up with gas, and where we saw all the cows being milked. Very fine Ayrshire cows, and nice dairymaids. It is all kept up just as the late Duke wished it. We came home at half past seven. It never ceased raining. The Cathedral bell began quite unexpectedly to ring, or almost toll, at eight o'clock, which the Duchess told us was a very old custom – in fact, the curfew-bell. It sounds very melancholy. Dinner was just as yesterday.*

Returning to the Duchess's quarters at the farm after the tour, tea was served using Mrs Gillespie's china, which had been given to her as a wedding present. On learning this the Queen offered to remedy the situation and within a few weeks a fine, attractive tea service in a pretty wild strawberry design was delivered and much admired.

It was dark when they reached Dunkeld and still raining heavily. Here, beside the imposing entrance to the old Dunkeld House, the Queen paid a visit to the dairy, lit, even in those days, by gas, where she admired the fine herd of Ayrshire cows started by the 6th Duke and then famous throughout the country. Ann Reid, head dairymaid and her assistants, Martha Sellars and Mary Neil, were delighted for the chance to see the Queen. That night Alexander Stewart, the ground officer and William Pitcaithly, an under keeper, were on guard and they alone ensured the safekeeping of the Queen.

The 'melancholy' tolling of the cathedral bell had been noticed by the Queen. This was rung at eight o'clock at night as the ancient curfew and again at six in the morning to signal the start of the working day.

> *Wednesday, October 11.*
>
> *Another wretchedly wet morning. Was much distressed to find that poor Brown's legs had been dreadfully cut by the edge of his wet kilt on Monday, just at the back of the knee, and he said nothing about it; but to-day one became so inflamed, and swelled so much, that he could hardly move. The doctor said he must keep it up as much as possible, and walk very little, but did not forbid his going out with the carriage, which he wished to do. I did not go out in the morning, and decided to remain till Friday, to give the weather a chance. It cleared just before luncheon, and we agreed to take a drive, which we were able to do almost without any rain.*

For the third day in a row it rained heavily and, with an apparent promise of better weather to come, Queen Victoria decided to prolong her stay by a day and not return to Balmoral until the Friday. She loved the total privacy of the Cottage and also 'the respectful conduct of the inhabitants of the town, who did not in any way obtrude themselves, or crowd on the Highway to see the Queen drive past'. Because of this, she willingly agreed to drive

Polney Loch in 1858

through the town to give the townsfolk a chance to see her and Mr Carrington, factor of the Atholl Estates, duly informed Mr Conacher, the Town Bailie, of her plans.

> *At half-past three we drove out just as yesterday. There was no mist, so that, though there was no sunshine, we could see and admire the country, the scenery of which is beautiful. We drove a mile along the Blair Road to Polney Loch, where we entered the woods, and skirting the loch, drove at the foot of Craig y Barns on grass drives – which were very deep and rough, owing to the wet weather, but extremely pretty – on to the Loch Ordie road. After ascending this for a little way we left it, driving all round Cally Loch (there are innumerable lochs) through Cally Gardens along another fine but equally rough wood drive, which comes out on the Blairgowrie high road. After this we drove round the three Lochs of the Lowes – viz. Craig Lush, Butterstone, and the Loch of the Lowes itself (which is the largest). They are surrounded by trees and woods, of which there is no end, and are very pretty.*

In the hope of seeing a little more of the beautiful Perthshire scenery, Lady Ely and General Grey set off after lunch and drove north to Pitlochry and the Pass of Killiecrankie. A little later the Queen and the Duchess set off in the phaeton, followed by Princess Helena and Amelia MacGregor in the sociable. They turned off the highway after a mile or so along the grassy track beside Polney Loch, a small sheet of water nestling below the craggy heights of Craig a Barns. It is a quiet and peaceful spot with trees and rocks intermingling at the water's edge, but this tranquillity was often shattered in winter by the shouts and cries of curlers, as the loch was one of the rinks of the Dunkeld Curling Club, formed in 1834. The Queen's route passed close by the club pavilion, which still stands at the start of a picturesque three-mile drive through natural woodlands of oak, sycamore, fir and beech, along with more recently planted larch and spruce. Here also were juniper bushes, wild roses, blaeberries, holly and broom, all combining to give a variety of colour and texture for many months in the year.

Cally Loch was formerly a peat moss and was landscaped with rhododendron bushes along its edge while the loch was planted with water lilies, with a broad green walk round its perimeter. Nowadays the loch is neglected, but in summer the red masses of rhododendron and brilliant yellow blooms of azaleas hide much that is unsightly. The woodland track comes out on the Blairgowrie road at the Crieff Gate below the hill of the same name and from here the royal party toured round the three lochs of Craiglush, Butterstone and Lowes. The Loch of the Lowes, three miles in circumference, is the largest of the three and is a fine expanse of water with a profusion of birch, alder and hazel growing on its banks. Writing of fishing on the loch in 1807, the Atholl factor recorded a catch of one salmon; four trout, one of 5lb, two of 4lb and two each of 2lb ('I never saw finer trout'); twenty-four perch; twenty-four eels and two pike. The Loch of the Lowes is now owned by the Scottish Wildlife Trust, who have constructed a hide at the west end of the loch to allow many types of waterfowl – including in some years the ospreys which have nested here – to be viewed unobserved.

We came back by the Blairgowrie road and drove through Dunkeld (the people had been so discreet and quiet, I said I would do this), crossing over the bridge (where twenty two years ago we were met by twenty of the Athole Highlanders, who conducted us to the entrance of the grounds), and proceeded by the upper road to the Rumbling Bridge, which is Sir William Stewart of Grandtully's property. We got out here and walked to the bridge, under which the Braan flowed over the rocks most splendidly; and swollen by the rain, it came down in an immense volume of water with a deafening noise. Returning thence we drove through the village of Inver to the Hermitage on the banks of the Braan, which is Dunkeld property. This is a little house full of looking-glasses, with painted walls, looking on another fall of the Braan, where we took tea almost in the dark. It was built by James, the second Duke of Athole in the last century.

By this time the weather had improved and as Queen Victoria drove back through Dunkeld she acknowledged the crowds which had gathered along the main street and 'testified their loving respects by repeated bows and cheers and waving of handkerchiefs'. As she crossed the Dunkeld Bridge, the Queen reflected on the glory and pageantry of her triumphal entry to the town twenty-three years earlier, when she had been greeted by a guard of honour of Atholl Highlanders bearing their Lochaber axes. The party followed the old Crieff road, which stayed on the north bank of the Braan and passed through the trees below Craigvinean to the Rumbling Bridge, three miles from Dunkeld. The bridge is a single arch across a deep chasm and in times of spate the river thunders and roars as it plunges under the bridge to reach calmer and more placid waters below. In the old days there was no parapet to protect travellers and it must have been a terrifying experience to cross it on a dark and windy night.

According to Amelia MacGregor, there was at the bridge:

> . . . A curious looking person who seemed somewhat eccentric stood all the time not far off with his hat in his hand but altho' he had not the discretion to withdraw he appeared to be perfectly harmless. John Grant addressed him in English and Gaelic but without eliciting a response. It was afterwards ascertained however that he was a Stranger of rather weak mind staying in the neighbourhood.

The Hermitage

The ladies retraced their route to the Hermitage, sometimes called Ossian's Hall, where tea was taken. The 2nd Duke had built the Hermitage in 1757 on a rocky outcrop which afforded magnificent views of the waterfall on the Braan. It was cleverly constructed in such a way that the full magnificence of the falls was not revealed and therefore appreciated, until one was actually inside the building. Originally it had a mirrored interior, which reflected the falls in such a way as to give the impression of water flowing all round, with sometimes even leaping salmon reflected on the walls. The building is the focal point of a tree garden laid out with exotic species like monkey puzzle, cedar of Lebanon and silver fir, while a simple stone bridge spans the gorge below the viewpoint. Ossian's Cave, a romantic folly artfully constructed from a group of large boulders, is a few hundred yards upstream. Within a few years of the Queen's visit the Hermitage was damaged by explosives and although the identity of the vandals was never discovered, it was suspected that they were connected with the Dunkeld Bridge Pontage Tax controversy.

> We drove back through Dunkeld again, the people cheering. Quite fair. We came home at half past six o'clock. Lady Ely and General Grey dined with us. After dinner only the Duchess came to the drawing-room and read to us again. Then I wrote, and Grant waited instead of Brown, who was to keep quiet on account of his leg.

The Queen was very concerned about John Brown all that day – her diary describes how during the long wet march on the Monday, his kilt had chafed his legs which became very sore and inflamed, making him lame. He was treated by Dr Charles Jack and the Queen insisted that he should rest. That evening, Lady Ely and General Grey joined with the Duchess and Miss MacGregor in dining with the Queen and Princess. John Conacher, son of the Town Bailie, along with James Robertson, tenant of the Lowes Farm, mounted guard.

> *Thursday, October 12.*
>
> A fair day, with no rain, but alas! no sunshine. Brown's leg was much better, and the doctor thought he could walk over the hill to-morrow.
>
> Excellent breakfasts, such splendid cream and butter! The Duchess has a very good cook, a Scotchwoman, and I thought how dear Albert would have liked it all.

He always said things tasted better in small houses. There were several Scotch dishes, two soups, and the celebrated 'haggis', which I tried last night, and really liked it very much. The Duchess was delighted at my taking it.

The plain fare of home-produced butter and cream, soups and haggis delighted the royal taste and the Queen could not help thinking on how much Prince Albert would have relished this home cooking. The contrast between the grandeur of Windsor and the simple food at the 'Cottage' all contributed to the great enjoyment of her stay in Dunkeld.

Dunkeld Cathedral

At a quarter past twelve Lenchen and I walked with the Duchess in the grounds and saw the Cathedral, part of which is converted into a parish church, and the other part is a most picturesque ruin. We saw the tomb of the Wolf of Badenoch, son of King Robert the Second. There are also other monuments, but in a very dilapidated state. The burying-ground is inside and south of the Cathedral.

In the late morning the Queen, the Duchess and Princess Helena walked in the grounds and visited the cathedral. Its site is associated with a remote period of the ecclesiastical history of Scotland and it is probable that a Celtic community was already settled here in the ninth century, when Iona was no longer safe from Viking invasion and Dunkeld was chosen as the centre of Scottish Christianity.

In 1689 Highland supporters of the Stuart dynasty defended Dunkeld against the forces of William and Mary. Lead from the cathedral roof was turned into shot and many of the pews were removed to set fire to houses in the town held by Highland troops. By the end of the battle the cathedral and many of the houses were in ruins. In 1815 the 4th Duke raised £5,000 and the government donated £1,000 to furnish an extensive rebuilding programme. The choir presbytery, the oldest part of the cathedral, was restored to serve as the parish church and retains much of its thirteenth-century character. Immediately behind the altar screen is the tomb of the Wolf of Badenoch, a recumbent figure in full armour with arms folded, which the Queen came to see on her visit to the cathedral. The Wolf, Alexander Stewart, son of King Robert II of Scotland, was one of the most feared and hated men of his time, with a reputation that outlived him for centuries, one of his more notorious deeds being the destruction of Elgin Cathedral. After due penance he received absolution from the Archbishop of St Andrews. The nave of the cathedral has never been restored and in it are the 'monuments' mentioned in the Queen's diary. One of these is the tomb of Bishop Robert Cardney in the south aisle, who, with Bishop Lauder, was responsible for the massive cathedral building operations in the fifteenth century, while another is a statue of the early fourteenth-century Bishop, William Sinclair, in the north aisle.

We walked along the side of the river Tay, into which the River Braan flows, under very fine trees, as far as the American garden, and then round by the terrace overlooking the park, on which the tents were pitched at the time of the great déjeuner that the Duke, then Lord Glenlyon, gave us in 1842, which was our first acquaintance with the Highlands and Highland customs; and it was such a fine sight! Oh! and here we were together – both widows! We came back through the kitchen-garden by half-past one o'clock.

Queen Victoria's walk led her from the Cottage with its exquisite flower garden to beyond the Cathedral, where she walked along the banks of the Tay until she and the Duchess reached the American Garden on the Haugh of the Cummings. This had been laid out in the previous century with several varieties of rhododendron bushes, hardy evergreens and summer-flowering kalmia shrubs, beautifully sheltered by mature trees to form a secluded retreat. It had a grotto, a Chinese temple, various seats and summerhouses to afford the best views of the Tay and also a turret called 'the Fort', 'militarised' with thirty wooden cannons. It was a simple square tower, with the north wall blank and an archway in the other three sides, providing views across the river. It was time to reminisce as the Queen and Duchess approached the park, scene of the Highland welcome and lavish entertainment of 1842 and no doubt the shared memories of happier times and mutual sorrow helped to strengthen the bond between them. They returned by way of the kitchen garden, behind a high bank of shrubbery where there were vineries, greenhouses and a peach house further up, enclosed within a high wall.

That morning Princess Helena, with Miss MacGregor, visited the stables next to the dairy and, passing through William Stewart's Gate, walked through the town to the Duchess Anne School, a girls' school opened in 1855 by means of money donated by the Duchess. The Princess was introduced to Miss Arneil, the teacher and inspected the pupils' work.

After the usual luncheon, drove with Lenchen, the Duchess, and Miss MacGregor, at twenty minutes to four, in her sociable to Loch Ordie, by the lakes of Rotmell and Dowally through the wood, being the road by which we ought to have come the first night when we lost our way. It was cold, but the sky was quite bright, and it was a fine evening; and the lake wooded to the water's edge and skirted by distant hills, looked very pretty. We took a short row on it in a 'coble' rowed by the head keeper, Gregor McGregor. We took tea under the trees. The evening was very cold, and it was getting rapidly dark. We came back safely by the road the Duchess had wished to come the other night, but which her coachman did not think safe because of the precipices! We got home at nine.

On the way to Loch Ordie for the afternoon excursion the Queen stopped at the Kennel Lodge to speak to Mrs Agnes Brearley, formerly Miss Fisher, who had been a schoolmistress in the Lochnagar Girls' School near Balmoral. Agnes had lost her husband, an excise officer, only four months earlier, and her mother was the widow of James Fisher who had been the farm grieve at St Colme's for many years. It was a very touching meeting, as Amelia MacGregor recorded:

It was a sad and touching interest to see together the Queen, the Duchess, Mrs Fisher, Mrs Brearley all so recently widowed. Mrs Fisher the eldest not yet old, and Agnes the youngest, only 23.

After speaking a few kind words to the mother and daughter, the royal party drove on to Loch Ordie, following the road the coachman should have taken on the previous Monday and passing the two beautiful small lochs of Rotmell and Dowally. At Loch Ordie the Queen went for a row in a Tay coble, a short, flat-bottomed type of boat used for salmon fishing and also as a ferry boat. The Queen described her first experience in a coble on Loch Insh in her entry of Tuesday 4 September 1860:

> The Ferry was a very rude affair; it was like a boat or cobble, but we could only stand on it, and it was moved at one end by two long oars plied by the ferryman and Brown, and at the other end by a long sort of beam.

Tea, prepared by Mrs McCall, was then taken on a grassy bank beside the lodge, overlooking the loch. The return drive along the grassy track, which had been the Duchess's preferred route the previous Monday, was quickly achieved and made them all wonder how they could have encountered such problems only a few days earlier.

> Only the Duchess and Miss MacGregor dined with us. The Duke's former excellent valet, Christie (a Highlander, and now the Duchess's house-steward) and George McPherson, piper, and Charles McLaren, footman, two nice good-looking Highlanders in the Athole tartan, waited on us. The Duchess read again a little to us after dinner.

That night John MacGregor and James Gillespie kept guard.

Return to Balmoral

> Friday, October 13.
> Quite a fine morning, with bright gleams of sunshine lighting up everything. The piper played each morning in the garden during breakfast. Just before we left at ten, I planted a tree, and spoke to an old acquaintance, Willie Duff, the Duchess's fisherman, who had formerly a very long black beard and hair, which are now quite grey. Mr Carrington, who has been Secretary to the Athole family for four generations, was presented.

The day was fine for the return journey and, as on every morning during her stay, William Ross, the Balmoral piper, played during breakfast. Shortly after, the Queen planted an Atlas cedar sapling of about 2ft (60cm) in height on the lawn opposite the south porch of the cathedral, close to the bowling green. After the planting she was heard to say: 'I think that will do.' When this tree was examined fifteen years later it had reached a height of 17ft (5m).

Among those presented to the Queen before her departure was her old acquaintance Willie Duff and they chatted for a few minutes about their previous meeting in 1844. Mr Carrington was also presented. He had worked for four of the Dukes of Atholl, beginning as secretary to the 4th Duke: he was appointed factor during the lifetime of the 5th Duke, served under the 6th and by the time of the Queen's visit was employed by the 7th. The eight men who had acted as sentries during the week were drawn up in line outside the Cottage, and each was presented with a photograph of the Queen. The Duchess had them framed, knowing that they would be 'highly valued during their lives and handed down hereafter as heirlooms'.

> *General Grey, Lady Ely and Miss MacGregor had gone on a little while before us. Lenchen and I, with the Duchess went in the sociable with four horses (Brown and Grant on the box). The weather was splendid, and the view as we drove along the Inverness Road – which is the road to Blair – with all the mountains rising in the distance, was beautiful.*

The advance party set off half an hour earlier, arranging to meet the Queen at Kindrogan, then she and Princess Helena, both dressed in black riding habits, drove off in the sociable drawn by four magnificent greys with outriders. The Duchess had thrown open the grounds, and the inhabitants of the town turned out to witness the Queen's departure, shouting, 'Haste ye back' and 'Welcome back.'

> *We passed through the village of Ballinluig, where there is a railway station, and a quarter of a mile below which the Tay and the Tummel unite, at a place called Logierait. All these names were familiar to me from our stay in 1844. We saw the place where the monument to the Duke is to be raised, on an eminence above Logierait. About eleven miles from Dunkeld, just below Croftinloan (Captain Jack Murray's), we took post horses. You could see Pitlochry in the distance to the left.*

They took the highway on the east bank of the Tay, retracing their journey of 1844, and passed through Ballinluig. Its railway station was on the main line to Inverness and at the start of the branch line to Aberfeldy. The spot on Tom na Croiche ('gallows knoll') where a monument to the 6th Duke was to be erected above Logierait, near the site of an old castle built by Robert II in the fourteenth century, was pointed out to the Queen. This monument, now almost totally enclosed by trees, is a richly sculptured Celtic cross designed by Rowland Anderson, an architect from Edinburgh. It carries the inscription:

TO THE MEMORY OF
GEORGE AUGUSTUS FREDERICK JOHN MURRAY
SIXTH DUKE OF ATHOLE K.T.
WHO DIED XVI JANUARY 1864, AGED XLIX
ERECTED 1866
BY THE INHABITANTS OF ATHOLE AND NUMEROUS FRIENDS, IN
TESTIMONY OF THEIR REGARD AND ESTEEM FOR HIS
CHARACTER, AND IN MEMORIAL OF THEIR GRIEF
FOR THE LOSS THE COUNTRY HAS SUSTAINED BY HIS DEATH.

As the Queen paused to admire the view along Strathtay she saw Dr Irvine, the medical adviser to the Atholl family and knowing of his devoted attention to the late Duke during his

chestnut and some copper beeches in the garden. The oldest part of the house dates from about 1700 and was built by William Small, an ancestor of Patrick Small Keir. During the nineteenth century a new frontage and wings were added and the house considerably enlarged as the family prospered. In 1963 Kindrogan was bought by the Scottish Field Studies Association and is now a residential field study centre.

The royal party crossed the River Ardle by means of an old stone bridge and crossed the highway at the East Lodge near the village of Enochdhu, a small hamlet which has changed little since Queen Victoria saw it.

Dirnanean

Once across the river the party entered the Dirnanean estate, owned by Mr James Small. By the 1860s the estate had been in the hands of the Small family for nearly 300 years, having passed from father to son for nine generations. A charter of 1588 records that Andrew Small was granted the lands in Strathardle by John, the 5th Stewart Earl of Atholl. Ardle's Grave, the burial place of a chief of the Caledonians called Ard-fhuil, is beside the entrance lodge. The grave is 16ft (4.8m) long, with a large headstone at one end and a smaller stone at the other and is reputed to be where Ardle and a faithful henchman lie buried with their feet towards each other.

The party rode up the steep drive to Dirnanean House, white harled, imposing in appearance and situated on a high bank overlooking the glen. The Queen had insisted that there should be no advance notice of her journey and indeed, the exact route had only been agreed the previous day. A result of this was that Mr James Small was not at home, being away at the Perth Hunt, though the Queen remembered meeting his father, a large and heavy man, at Dunkeld in 1842. Mrs Small had died two years earlier and the only member of the family at home was James's sister, who was so ill that she could only gaze from a window. She did however, arrange for five Dirnanean men to guide the party across the hill and they were drawn up in line on the lawn in front of the house, 'all with the soldierly, yet free bearing so natural to Highlanders'. Two of the Dirnanean men took the lead and set off up the hill road to the Spittal of Glenshee, a distance of five miles, where carriages were waiting for the final part of the return journey to Balmoral.

We turned over the hill from here, through a wild, heathery glen, and then up a grassy hill called the Larich, just above the Spital. Looking back the view was splendid, one range of hills behind the other, of different shades of blue. After we had passed the summit, we stopped for our tea, about twenty minutes to four, and seated ourselves on the grass, but had to wait for some time till a kettle arrived which had been forgotten, and had to be sent for from the Spital. This caused some delay. At length, when tea was over, we walked down a little way, then rode. It was really most distressing to me to see what pain poor Brown suffered, especially in going up and down the hill. He could not go fast, and walked lame, but would not give in. His endurance on this occasion showed a brave heart indeed, for he resisted all attempts at being relieved, and would not relinquish his charge.

The hill road passed through the farm steading and then deteriorated into a rough peat track, sometimes of soft grass cut by drains, while other parts were steep and rocky. The steading comprised a range of buildings standing a few hundred yards behind Dirnanean House, described thus in an 1880 account:

The byres and stables are kept remarkably tidy being paragons of cleanliness in their way; while the dairy etc., are a perfect treat. The various kinds of stock grace their habitation. The accommodation of the farm servants is really comfortable. The policy grounds are very tastefully laid out, and the avenue is one of the nicest to be seen. A fine burn runs along the east side of the steading, the mansion and the avenue and joins the Ardle at the village of Ennochdhu. The burn flows through a deep den, which is prettily laid out with walks and rockeries constructed with 'creature stones'. Here, also, there is a nice heather or summer house perched on a precipice, overhanging a still pool and from which a charming view is obtained of two small cascades. The approach is also very lovely. Ardil's grave is situated here.

Sandy McInnes, the Kindrogan head shepherd, had gone on ahead with General Grey to see him safely on his way and he now joined up with the party. He carried some provisions and cups and saucers from Kindrogan for a proposed tea stop on the journey, but the observant Amelia MacGregor realised they did not have a kettle. William Spalding, a Dirnanean shepherd and John Stewart volunteered to go on to the Spittal and borrow a kettle and, as Miss MacGregor observed:

. . . confidently announcing as they started that they would be back at the top of the larach in time to meet the Queen and the rapid manner in which they sprang over the heather left little doubt that no effort would be wanting on their part to accomplish their errand.

Amelia MacGregor's journal graphically describes the next part of the journey:

As the ascent continued, the road was very lovely with its foreground of brown heather, blue shallow streams and grey rocks and distant views of hills with melting outlines, but the most magnificent sight was from the summit of the ridge looking back over the path lately traversed – ranges of hills rising one above the other including an immense sweep of country and fading away in the distance till their outlines seemed to vanish in the evening sky. It was a glorious scene! Looking forwards a rather wide glen opened out from amidst steep grassy hills – the burn ran winding through it towards the Inn of the Spittal Village, the smoke from whence curled gently upwards and beyond that to the left were the Aberdeen-shire hills of conical shapes, and the steep carriage road leading to that awkward turn of ill repute, 'the Devil's Elbow'. To the right of the Spittal cultivated fields and a broad flat stretched away towards the Lowlands.

Overlooking the Spittal

At four o'clock the travellers stopped at the top of the pass called the Lairig at 2,100ft (641m), overlooking the Spittal of Glenshee. The two volunteers were seen clambering back up the path with a kettle and a bundle of kindling wood. Mr James Small's butler, McKay, built up a fire 'at a heap of stones where the Highlanders were wont to have their fireplace'. Under Miss MacGregor's supervision the kettle was soon boiling and refreshing tea was enjoyed by every-one. Queen Victoria and Princess Helena sat on a plaid spread on the grass and, as it was getting cold, the Queen drank a little hot toddy and insisted it should be offered to everyone in the party! After tea the Queen walked down the hill to within a mile of the Spittal, where she and the other ladies remounted their ponies and rode the rest of the way to the hotel.

Queen Victoria was still most concerned about the well-being of John Brown, who was still suffering from swollen and inflamed legs and could hardly walk, but 'he had bravely walked on all day leading the Queen's pony'.

> We took leave of the dear kind Duchess and Miss MacGregor, who were going back to Kindrogan, and got into the carriage. We were able to ascend the Devil's Elbow before it was really dark, and we got to Castleton at half-past seven, where we found our own horses, and reached Balmoral at half-past eight.

Carriages were waiting for them as they arrived at the Invercauld Arms Hotel, as the Spittal Inn was formerly known and after fond farewells the Queen and her party departed along the road to Castletown of Braemar and finally Balmoral. Miss MacGregor observed that:

> A strange blank for a moment fell on the hearts of all the Queen's Athole following, as the Royal Carriage was seen disappearing in the distance; but it was very soon succeeded by excitement and delight at the success of the expedition.

Return to Kindrogan

The Duchess and Miss MacGregor went into the hotel where Mrs Grant, the kindly owner, plied them with sustaining negus (hot port, sweetened and spiced) and biscuits. They then remounted their ponies for the return journey to Kindrogan, just before six o'clock. By the time they arrived at the tea encampment at the top of the hill it was dark. The men chatted freely, some leading ponies and others walking in front, their sporrans turned round so that the white goatskin could be seen easily by those behind as a guide. During this journey Amelia MacGregor reflected on the events of the past few days, especially the journey back to Kindrogan and these thoughts are echoed in her journal:

> On this night every feeling harmonized with the scene – who knows what strange trage-dies may have been enacted on that very hill, how our ancestors may have fought and bled and died there, our Prince too may have wandered there, his only wealth those true

John Brown in 1865

Blair Castle in the 1860s

Queen Victoria and Princess Helena in 1863

The Hermitage, 'a little house full of looking glasses, with painted walls, looking on another fall of the Braan' – Queen Victoria

View from the Hermitage of the Braan in spate

Ann Reid, head dairymaid at Dunkeld with Colley Hill, the Ayrshire cow which took first prize at the English Agricultural Show in London in 1862

Willie Duff, 'now quite grey', with his grandson, Willie Heriot, described as 'an innocent'

The Maharajah Dhulep Singh, who leased Grandtully Castle in 1866

Queen Victoria at Balmoral in 1865

The 'wild moor' of Moulin. John Soutar perished near the house beside the tree

Kindrogan House

One of the cascades on the stream that flows through Dirnanean

Highland hearts which were his unto death. Another association now will be linked with that hill and retained in affectionate remembrance by Highlanders, no less true than their Fathers. An actual fact this time, a romance indeed but no dream. In after years it will be told how Scotland's widowed Queen, with her dutiful and loving Daughter crossed the hill attended only by three Scotch ladies, a Highland Laird and a trusty band of Highlanders, including her own Balmoral men . . . .

Our present Sovereign calls forth enthusiastic devotion by Her truthfulness, Her brave disregard of inconvenience, weather and discomfort and also by the sacredness of that great sorrow which has made Her tho' a Queen, a lonely and grief-stricken woman. Curious was the thought 'Here is one of the greatest Sovereigns of the World, over whose vast empire the sun never sets, riding along so simply: In no other country but Great Britain could such be possible.

Parts of the hill track were difficult, with deep potholes and ruts, but all reached the firmer peat road in safety and arrived at Dirnanean House at 7.30pm. Here the Duchess, Miss MacGregor and Mr Small Keir had tea with Miss Small, who was feeling better and was delighted to learn how useful her five men had been on the journey. After a short stay they rode off again, the two ladies enjoying Mr Small Keir's kind hospitality at Kindrogan, where they passed a pleasant evening discussing the activities of the day. Next morning the Duchess and Miss MacGregor returned to Dunkeld.

The very evening the Queen arrived back at Balmoral she scribbled a quick note of thanks to Duchess Anne:

Dearest kindest Duchess,
I cannot go to bed tonight without telling you of our safe arrival home at 8 – having got in there before dark. I cannot say how charmed Helena and I were with the trip and Miss MacGregor.

Two days later, Lady Ely wrote to the Duchess informing her that:

The Queen said She had enjoyed her visit beyond everything and spoke so much of your kindness and attention to her. I cannot tell you with how much affection the Queen spoke of you. Her Majesty was delighted with Miss MacGregor & said so much in her praise. We found all dressing & dining here for the ball at Abergeldie, so the Queen dined alone with Princess Helena & myself & the Queen talked of you all dinnertime . . . .

Even little Princess Beatrice, then aged eight, wrote on 16 October:

I thank you very much for the nice present you so kindly sent me, it looks so pretty on my table. I wish I had been with Mama to see you, she says it is such a pretty place.
Goodbye dear Duchess
I remain your
grateful little friend.

Finally, Princess Louise wrote to the Duchess and her letter contained a clue about their expectations for the following year.

> . . . *Mama and Helena were both enchanted with their visit and have been telling me a great deal about it. We had much finer weather on our trip than you and enjoyed ourselves immensely. Mama says kindly that next year if she comes and sees the dear Duchess again I will be taken, this thought pleases me very much.*
> *I am ever dearest Duchess your*
> *very affectionate friend*
>
> *Louise.*

Thus the seeds were sown for what was to be Queen Victoria's final visit to Highland Perthshire.

CHAPTER SIX

1866
Second Visit to the 'Cottage'

DUNKELD,
MONDAY 1–SATURDAY 6 OCTOBER

Towards the end of her stay in Dunkeld in 1865 Queen Victoria was already planning a return visit and in September of the following year General Grey started making arrangements for the journey. It was agreed that the royal party would stop on the road for lunch near the Spittal of Glenshee and, provided the weather was fine, take the hill track to Dirnanean. In a letter of 26 September 1866, General Grey indicated to Duchess Anne the Queen's views about where they should meet on the journey:

> . . . the Queen hopes you will not come all the way to the Spital to meet her on Monday – for if the day is not fine she thinks she will prefer driving round all the way. She prefers to lunch on the road before she gets to the Spital – as she did last year on the way to Kindrogan . . .

Two days later the Queen herself wrote to the Duchess concerning the journey, and also to make arrangements for her servant, Andrew Thomson and for a tea stop en route to Dunkeld.

> Your proposal for the lodging of Arthur I gladly accept. It will be very convenient. If A. Thomson could have a room in the Brick building where there is a fireplace – it would be a convenience in order to dry the cloaks etc. – in case of wet.
>
> The Hills are so wet from the great amount of rain that **Fealar** would not do besides it being rather longer than I feel up to. Should the weather be fine perhaps we may return that way – Tea had perhaps best be at or near Kindrogan and my baskets will come with me.
>
> If it should be wet – I shall drive the whole way & in that case I beg you not to ride over to the Spital. I wish also to mention that Brown would now wait at luncheon and dinner being an upper servant – unless he should be very tired and come in late. I have no objection to Mr Small's joining with us & shall be glad to see Mrs Keir at Kindrogan.

Amelia MacGregor (standing), serving tea to Duchess Anne and a friend outside the 'Cottage'

Duchess Anne was asked to make all the arrangements for the journey from Dirnanean to Dunkeld and, dreading a repeat of the previous year's fiasco, decided to keep to the highway over to Pitlochry and change horses at Ballinluig. The weekend before the royal visit, she and Amelia MacGregor stayed at Kindrogan and set off for the Spittal of Glenshee at eleven o'clock on the Monday, which 'dawned brightly and a more lovely autumn day could scarcely be found.' Patrick Small Keir and his son, William accompanied them, along with James Gillespie, the St Colme's farm grieve and young Gregor MacGregor. As they passed through the grounds of Dirnanean House, James Small, the proprietor, a lieutenant in the Atholl Highlanders joined them with three of his men. Their ride to the Spittal was uneventful and they arrived at the Invercauld Arms just after one o'clock.

The Queen's diary continues with the details of the journey:

> *Monday, October 1, 1866.*
> *A very fine morning. Got up earlier, and breakfasted earlier, and left at a quarter to ten with Louise and Janie Ely (attended by Brown and Grant as formerly); Arthur having gone on with General Grey. We met many droves of cattle on the road, as it was the day for the tryst at Castleton. It was very hot, the sun very bright, and the Cairn Wall looked wild and grand. But as we went on the sky became dull and overcast, and we almost feared there might be rain. We walked down the Devil's*

The Invercauld Arms, later renamed the Spittal of Glenshee Hotel

Elbow, and when within a mile and a half of the Spital we stopped and lunched in the carriage, and even sketched a little. A little way on the north side of the Spital were the ponies, Gordon for me, Brechin for Louise and Cromar for Janie Ely. There was a pony for Arthur, which he did not ride, and for Grant or any one who was tired. The dear Duchess of Athole and Miss MacGregor came to meet us here, and when we had reached the spot where the road turns up the hill, we found Mr Keir and his son, and Mr Small of Dirnanean – a strong good-looking, and pleasing person about thirty-two – and his men, the same two fine tall men, preceding us as last year.

General Grey and Prince Arthur travelled on ahead of Queen Victoria, arriving at the Spittal in time for lunch. Arthur was the Queen's third son, born in 1850 and she hoped he would 'wear the lily of a blameless life', trusting that the lily would never fade. He served in the army and later became the Duke of Connaught. Princess Louise, the Queen's fourth daughter born in 1848, was also in the party. She was described as a lively, sparkling girl with plenty of wit and talent, who married the Marquis of Lorne and through this became the Duchess of Argyll.

After half an hour the Queen's carriage was spied coming from the direction of the Devil's Elbow, by which time a small crowd had gathered to watch the royal progress. After fond greetings, the party mounted their ponies and set off up the hill road. Prince Arthur was

Prince Arthur, who came to Dunkeld with the Queen in 1866

prepared to walk the six miles to Kindrogan, asking John Grant to ride his pony while he strode alongside and 'did not seem in the least bit fatigued'.

> *It was a steep climb up the hill which we had then come down, and excessively hot. The views both ways beautiful, though not clear. The air was very heavy and oppressive. We went the same way as before, but the ground was very wet from the great amount of rain. We stopped a moment in passing, at Dirnanean, to speak to Miss Small, Mr Small's sister, a tall, stout young lady, and then went on to Kindrogan, Mr Keir's. All about here the people speak Gaelic, and there are a few who do not speak a word of English.*

The Hill Road to Kindrogan

It is a steep ascent to the pass at An Lairig, nearly 1,000ft (305m) being climbed in under a mile and Duchess Anne's pony Grouse 'was in a very restive mood and plunged very unpleasantly but Gillespie walked by his side.' Just about four o'clock the royal party reached Dirnanean where Miss Small was presented to the Queen, after which they rode downhill and across the River Ardle, to approach Kindrogan House from the east. Kindrogan is in the parish of Kirk-michael, then with a population of more than a thousand of whom almost a third spoke Gaelic and this probably accounts for the Queen's observations on this subject.

Soon after entering Mr Keir's grounds we got off our ponies, and went along a few yards by the side of the river Ardle to where Mr Keir had got a fire kindled and a kettle boiling, plaids spread and tea prepared. Mrs Keir and her two daughters were there. She is a nice quiet person, and was a Miss Menzies, daughter of Sir Neil Menzies, whom I saw at Taymouth in 1842.

Only we ladies remained. The tea over, we walked up to the house, which is a nice comfortable one. We waited here a little while, and I saw at the door Major Balfour of Fernie, the intended bridegroom of Mr Keir's youngest daughter.

Queen Victoria had already agreed to have tea outside at Kindrogan and, having dismounted, she walked down a little path off the drive to a birch glade beside the river. Here Mrs Keir, daughter of Sir Neil Menzies who had paraded with his clansmen at Taymouth in 1842, was preparing tea. She was assisted by her two daughters; Catherine, whom the Queen had met the previous year at Pitcarmick, and Jane Amelia, who was engaged to be married to Major Balfour of Fernie, who owned a 1,725-acre estate four miles west of Cupar in Fife and was present that day. The picnic scene, with the kettle boiling on the fire and plaids spread all around, 'had a very pretty effect with the water rippling below and a very clear well close at hand'. During tea the Queen accidentally broke a cup, and later made amends by replacing it with a complete service. Both broken cup and service are still treasured by the family. The tea party is commemorated by a plaque which reads: 'The Queen rested here and partook of tea on Her Majesty's way from Balmoral by the Spittal of Glenshee to Dunkeld. 1st October 1866.' Prince Arthur and General Grey had refreshments in the dining room and the Queen rested in the drawing room for a little while after tea.

At a little over a quarter-past five started in my sociable, with Louise and the Duchess. We came very fast and well with the Duchess's horses by exactly the same road we drove from Dunkeld last year. The horses were watered at the small halfway house of Ballinluig, and we reached Dunkeld in perfect safety at ten minutes past seven. I am where I was before. Louise in Lenchen's room, and Arthur in a room next to where Brown was before, and is now. All the rest the same, and snug, peaceful, comfortable.

Having said goodbye to the Small Keir family, the Queen, with Princess Louise and the Duchess, drove off in her sociable followed by Prince Arthur, Lady Ely, General Grey and Miss MacGregor in the Duchess's barouche, drawn by horses from Fishers Hotel, Pitlochry. They arrived at the 'Cottage' in Dunkeld just after seven o'clock to familiar surroundings – nothing had apparently changed – and the Queen was in the same bedroom as before, with Louise in the one previously occupied by Princess Helena.

Dunkeld, Tuesday, October 2.
Mild and muggy, the mist hanging on the hills. Breakfasted with the children. Andrew Thomson attends to Arthur. Emilie and Annie Macdonald are with me here;

> *they help Louise, who, however, is very handy and can do almost everything for herself.*
>
> *At half-past eleven I drove out alone with the Duchess through the woods to Polney, and then along the road, and turned in at Willie Duff's Lodge, and down the whole way along the river under splendid trees which remind me of Windsor Park. How dearest Albert would have admired them! We ended by a little walk, and looked into the old ruin.*

Next morning, a misty autumn one, the Queen and Duchess drove out from Dunkeld along the Blairgowrie road a little way and then turned off at Cally Lodge at the start of the right of way to Kirkmichael. They continued up the hill, passed Polney Loch and emerged on to the Inverness road, driving a couple of miles along it to Leadpettie Lodge, then home to Willie Duff, returning along by the river. They followed the line taken by General Wade's road in the 1720s. When they reached the American Garden the Queen and Duchess got out and walked back to the 'Cottage', taking another look in passing at the ruins of the house begun by the 4th Duke in 1828.

> *At twenty minutes to four we drove, the Duchess, Louise and I – Janie Ely and Miss MacGregor following – to Crieff-gate on the road of the Loch of the Lowes, where we got on ponies and rode for about an hour and a half through beautiful woods (saw a capercailzie, of which there are many here), but in a very thick mist (with very fine rain) which entirely destroyed anything but what was near. We came down to St Colme's, where we got off, but where again, like last year, we saw nothing of the beautiful view. Here we took tea out of the set I had given the Duchess. She has furnished all her rooms here so prettily. How Albert would have liked all this!*
>
> *Dinner as yesterday. Brown waited at dinner.*

That afternoon Queen Victoria and the ladies drove out again along the Blairgowrie road for a distance of two miles to the Crieff Gate, where they met up with John MacGregor and their ponies. With MacGregor acting as guide, they rode off through the Cally Woods up the road they had come down the previous year. Just after Cally Loch they turned right up the hill to pass Hatton, Birkenburn and Glackmill, a saw mill tenanted by Thomas Rattray. A little further on they passed the mill dam and then rode by lochs Dowally and Rotmell, before descending to the old Dunkeld road by the side of the stream that runs out of Loch Ordie. They reached St Colme's at five o'clock, in a light drizzle which did nothing to dampen the Queen's spirits. The Duchess's taste in furnishing her wing of the farm was admired by the Queen and tea was taken in the dining room from the wild strawberry design tea service which had been a present from the Queen. By this time the carriages had come round from the Crieff Gate and after tea they drove back to Dunkeld. Prince Arthur had been out fishing.

That afternoon arrangements were being made for a seventy-mile excursion for the following day and this required careful planning. General Grey arranged for fresh horses to be available at regular intervals and Mr Fisher of the Royal Hotel in Dunkeld was to supply the

Niel Gow's cottage in the last century

first change at Sketewan, beyond Balnaguard, while at Kenmore a change of horse would take the party to Tummel Bridge. There, horses supplied by Fishers Hotel of Pitlochry would be waiting to convey them as far as Ballinluig, where the final leg home would be made by the Duchess's own horses.

Great Excursion

> *Wednesday, October 3.*
>
> *Just returned from a beautiful and successful journey of seventy miles (in ten hours and a half). I will try and begin an account of it. At nine the Duchess sent up to say she thought the mist would clear off (it was much the same as yesterday), and to suggest whether we had not better try and go as far as her horses would take us, and return if it was bad. I agreed readily to this. Arthur left before our breakfast to go to the Pass of Killiecrankie with Lady Ely and General Grey. At a quarter past ten, well provided, we started, Louise, the Duchess, Miss MacGregor, and I (in our riding habits, as they take less room). The mist was very thick at first, and even accompanied by a little drizzling rain, so that we could see none of the distant hills and scenery. We crossed the Tay Bridge, drove through Little Dunkeld and along the Braan through Inver (where Niel Gow, the fiddler) lived, afterwards along the Tay opposite to St Colme's.*

Having crossed the Tay the party passed Little Dunkeld, a hamlet with a manse and the parish church rebuilt, in a green park beside the river studded with beech trees, in 1798. The church is a plain white building, surrounded by a graveyard in which is the final resting place of Niel Gow, the famous local violinist and composer of Scottish fiddle music. Half a mile brought them to Inver, which, as its name implies, is at the confluence of two rivers, in this case the Braan and the Tay. At that time the village was little more than a cluster of cottages, some thatched, others slated and some in ruins, straggling up the slope behind the old inn.

This village was home to Niel Gow, in his time supreme among Highland fiddlers. He was born in 1727 and lived for the eighty years of his life in the same cottage which, though much altered, still survives as a private house. It was the birthplace of his four children, of whom Nathaniel was a masterly fiddle player, some say even greater than his father. A bronze plaque to their memory was unveiled by Katherine, the 8th Duchess of Atholl in 1949.

Robert Burns met Niel Gow, then in his sixtieth year, during his Highland journey in 1787 when they were both guests at breakfast with Dr Stewart (of the Bonskeid family) in Dunkeld. In his notes on the tour, Burns describes the scene thus:

> *Friday – Breakfast with Dr Stewart. Neil Gow plays; a short stout-built honest Highland*
> *figure, with his greyish hair shed on his honest social brow; an interesting face, marking*
> *strong sense, kind open-heartedness, mixed with unmistrusting simplicity.*

The Atholl family were patrons of Niel Gow and took him to London, where he quickly acquired a high reputation as a player of reels and strathspeys, his fiddling producing an 'electrifying' effect on the dancers. He composed over eighty tunes, many of which are still loved and played.

Before leaving Inver, Robert Burns visited the old inn and scratched a few lines on the parlour window:

> *Ye gods, ye gave to me a wife out o' your grace and pleasure,*
> *To be the partner of my life, and I was glad to have her;*
> *But if your Providence Divine for better things design her,*
> *T' obey your will, at any time, I'm willing to resign her.*

These ironical words apparently came from the lips of the landlord, inspired it seems by the scolding tongue of his wife! Charles Macintosh, the well-known Perthshire naturalist, was born in 1839 in a cottage very near Niel Gow's. As a little boy, Charles was taken by his mother to the roof of the Duke of Atholl's Arms, where he watched the royal procession pass along the High Street in 1842. They saw the Queen pass by again in the afternoon on her way to Taymouth Castle, where Charles' father performed with his violin later that evening.

> *Four miles from Dunkeld, at Inchmagranachan Farm, the Highlands are supposed*
> *to begin, and this is one of the boundaries of Athole. We drove through some*
> *beautiful woods – oak and beech with brushwood, reminding one of Windsor Park –*
> *overtopped by rocks. A mile further Dalguise begins (the property of Mr Stewart, now*

at the Cape of Good Hope), which is remarkable for two large orchards at either end, the trees laden with fruit in a way that reminded me of Germany. Kinnaird is next, the jointure house of the late Lady Glenlyon (mother to the late Duke). Just beyond this the Tummel and Tay join at the point of Logierait.

The royal route followed the road along the west bank of the Tay through natural woodland of oak, ash, beech and sycamore and reached Inchmagranachan, a large farm built below Craigvinean Forest at the start of the last century. Before the forest was planted several settlements were scattered along the open hillside and when these were abandoned the large farm was built. These lands were granted to Sir Thomas Hunter by the Bishop of Dunkeld in a charter in 1501 and were later purchased by the Marquis of Atholl in 1684.

Next the royal party passed Dalguise, which was acquired by Gregory, the first Bishop of Dunkeld, around 1060, later becoming a stronghold of the Stewarts from 1543. The laird in 1785 was Charles Stewart and he was succeeded by his son, John, who was sent to the Cape of Good Hope in 1829 as High Sheriff of the colony. Dalguise means 'haugh of the fir trees' and was described by Thomas Hunter in 1883 as being:

. . . one of the most thickly wooded estates in the country, very little of the timber having been cut for a long series of years. The trees in the garden are purely ornamental and the most worthy of notice are three gigantic Araucarias planted about 1845.

Within a few years of Queen Victoria's visit Dalguise House was leased to Mr Rupert Potter, whose daughter Beatrix spent many summers here during her father's ten-year lease between 1872 and 1882.

We now entered Strath Tay, still the Duke of Athole's property on the side along which we drove. The Tay is a fine large river; there are many small properties on the opposite side in the woods. The mist was now less thick and there was no rain, so that all the near country could be well seen. Post horses from Fisher of Castleton's brother, the innkeeper at Dunkeld, were waiting for us at Skituan, a little beyond Balnaguard (where we changed horses in 1842, and this was the very same road we took then). Now an unsightly and noisy railroad runs along this beautiful glen, from Dunkeld as far as Aberfeldy. We passed, close to the road, Grandtully Castle, belonging to Sir William Stewart, and is rented by the Maharajah Duleep Singh. It is a curious old castle, much in the style of Abergeldie, with an avenue of trees leading up to it.

Yet again the Queen records her disdain of that modern form of transport, the railway, although it must have greatly improved her comfort in travelling long distances. Opposite Dalguise she may well have noticed the striking bridge carrying the Highland Line across the Tay. This is a latticed iron viaduct, 360ft (110m) in span, resting on stone piers and flanked at each end by handsome masonry towers.

The royal party entered Strathtay opposite Logierait and stopped to change horses at

Sketewan. After a few miles they passed by Grandtully Castle, a Stewart house since the close of the fourteenth century which has only recently passed out of Stewart hands. It was built in 1560, when it consisted of two five-storey towers, but it was considerably extended in the next century when gables and other architectural features were added. The original castle had been much closer to the Tay, but was abandoned when one of the early lairds was shot from the opposite river bank while standing at his front door. Grandtully Castle was described by Hugh Macmillan at the turn of the century as:

> . . . a venerable and stately pile, surrounded by ancestral trees, chiefly elms and sycamores, which partially screen it from the view of passers-by, but enclose it in a haunt of immemorial peace.

In 1866 it was leased for the shooting to the Maharajah Dhulep Singh, who became a personal friend of the Royal Family.

At Aberfeldy, a pretty village opposite to Castle Menzies, one or two people seemed to know us. We now came in among fine high-wooded hills, and here it was much clearer. We were in the Breadalbane property and approaching Taymouth. We passed to the left, Bolfrax, where Lord Breadalbane's factor still lives, and to the right the principal lodge of Taymouth, which I so well remember going in by; but as we could not have driven through the grounds without asking permission and becoming known, which for various reasons we did not wish, we decided on not attempting it, and contented ourselves with getting out at a gate, close to a small fort, into which we were admitted by a woman from the gardener's house, close to which we stopped, and who had no idea who we were. We got out and looked down from this height upon the house below, the mist having cleared away sufficiently to show us everything; and here unknown, quite in private I gazed, not without deep inward emotion, on the scene of our reception, twenty-four years ago, by dear Lord Breadalbane in a princely style, not to be equalled for grandeur and poetic effect! Albert and I were only twenty-three, young and happy. How many are gone who were with us then! I was very thankful to have seen it again. It seemed unaltered. Everything was dripping from the mist. Taymouth is twenty-two miles from Dunkeld.

Aberfeldy consisted at that time of a long main street with one or two side streets running off a little square in the middle of the town. It was a thriving place and a popular summer resort with its local beauty spot, the Falls of Moness, whose banks were formerly clothed in graceful birch trees and from which it received the name 'The Birks of Aberfeldy'. These were made famous by Robert Burns on his 1787 tour in his poem:

> *The braes ascend like lofty wa's,*
> *The foaming stream deep-roaring fa's,*
> *O'erhung wi' fragrant spreading shaws,*
> *The Birks of Aberfeldy.*

The hoary cliffs are crown'd wi' flowers,
While o'er the linn the burnie pours,
And, rising, weets wi' misty showers
The Birks of Aberfeldy . . . .

Half way between Aberfeldy and Kenmore is the fine mansion house of Bolfracks standing out against the trees, home at the time of the Queen's 1866 visit to Lord Breadalbane's factor. Two miles further on are the standing stones of Croftmoraig, which were pointed out to the Queen. This is one of the most complete groups of standing stones in Scotland, comprising three concentric circles round an artificial mound. The largest stones are in the inner circle and the smallest on the outside. Present day archaeological opinion dates them at between 3,000 and 2,000BC.

Return to Taymouth – Incognito

On this journey, as on many others, the Queen's desire was for anonymity so that she could avoid fuss and crowds of sightseers. Not wishing to let her presence be made known at Taymouth, she elected to stop outside the grounds and look down, unobserved, on the Castle with her own private thoughts and memories of the splendours of 1842.

> *We got into the carriage again, the Duchess this time sitting near to me to prevent our appearance creating suspicion as to my being there. We drove on a short way through splendid woods with little waterfalls, and then turned into the little village of Kenmore, where a tryst was being held, through the midst of which we had to drive; but the people only recognised the Duchess. There was music going on, things being sold at booths, and on the small sloping green near the church cattle and ponies were collected – a most picturesque scene.*
>
> *Immediately after this we came upon the bridge, and Loch Tay, with its wooded banks, clear and yet misty, burst into view. This again reminded me of the past – of the row up the loch, which is sixteen miles long, in 1842, in several boats, with pibrochs playing, and the boatmen singing wild Gaelic songs. The McDougall steered us then, and showed us the real Brooch of Lorne taken from Robert Bruce.*
>
> *To the right we could see the grounds and fine park, looking rather like an English one. We stopped at Murray's Lodge, but instead of changing horses here, drove five miles up the loch, which was quite clear, and the stillness so great that the reflection on the lake's bosom was as strong as though it were a real landscape. Here we stopped, and got out and sat down on the shore of the loch, which is covered with fine quartz, of which we picked up some; took our luncheon about half-past one, and then sketched. By this time the mist had given way to the sun, and the lake, with its richly wooded banks and changing foliage, looked beautiful.*

After a further mile the party entered the picturesque village of Kenmore, to find a fair in progress. This local fair took place on the first Wednesday of October, before the Falkirk

Tryst. These famous trysts for cattle and horses took place on the second Tuesday and Wednesday of the months of August, September and October. Kenmore had grown since the Queen's first visit and now boasted a steamer link with Killin at the top end of Loch Tay. On crossing the Kenmore Bridge the vista up Loch Tay, with Ben Lawers in the distance, filled her gaze, while to the right she had a view of the immaculate grounds and avenues of the castle. The party drove along the lochside, passing the largest crannog, or artificial lake dwelling, in Loch Tay. This island has a causeway linking it with the shore which is visible in dry summers. The first record of the island appears in 1122, when King Alexander I of Scotland stayed there with his queen, Sybilla, who took ill and died. She was buried on the island, and to consecrate her burial the king granted the land to the monks of Scone Abbey. The little island became a monastery and the foreshore opposite became the monastery garden, planted with fruit trees. By the end of the fifteenth century it was in the hands of the Campbells of Glenorchy, where they remained for sixty years until Colin Campbell built Balloch Castle, the forerunner of Taymouth Castle.

The royal travellers stopped for lunch near Fearnan, four miles along the loch, which at one time was part of the lands of the Robertsons of Struan. Five hundred years ago they were great landowners in the area, with their property being created a Barony in 1451 through a royal charter of King James II. The old village of Fearnan was down by the lochside, where a number of houses fringed the pebbly shore.

Glen Lyon

At half-past two we re-entered our carriage, the horses having been changed, and drove back up a steep hill, crossing the river Lyon and going into Glenlyon, a beautiful wild glen with high green hills and rocks and trees, which I remember quite well driving through in 1842 – then also on a misty day: the mist hung over, and even in some places below the tops of the hills. We passed several small places – Glenlyon House, the property of F. G. Campbell of Troup. To the left also Fortingal village – Sir Robert Menzies' – and a new place called Dunaven House. Small, picturesque, and very fair cottages were dotted about, and there were others in small clusters; beautiful sycamores and other trees were to be seen near the riverside.

The road from the lochside leads up a narrow glen to the pass, from where a magnificent view is gained of the River Lyon breaking through precipitous hills to reach an open strath before its confluence with the Tay. After crossing the Bridge of Lyon, Queen Victoria drove past the site of an old camp, reputedly an outpost of the Roman army 2,000 years ago. There is a curious, longstanding tradition that Pontius Pilate was born here, since his father was supposed to have been sent on a peace mission to the local king whose fortress was nearby and Pilate was born in the camp while negotiations were continuing.

It is a short distance to Glenlyon House built by John Campbell in 1722. The 'Stone of Virtue', Clach Bhuaidh, was kept here – after it was immersed in water, any man sprinkled with water from it was believed to be invincible. This was done to all the men of Glenlyon before they joined Bonnie Prince Charlie in 1745, except for one, a tailor and he was killed at Culloden, while all the others returned safely. The laird in the 1860s was Francis William Garden-Campbell who held over 10,000 acres in Glenlyon as well as an estate of comparable size in Troup, Banffshire. It remained in Campbell hands until 1885, when it was sold to Sir Donald Currie, owner of the Union Castle shipping line.

Fortingall village is just a few hundred yards further on, and in the last century contained a hotel, a meal mill and saw mill, a shop, a church and a small cluster of houses around it. At the start of this century Sir Donald Currie built the thatched cottages for which unusual feature the village is best known, and many of the old crofts and farms disappeared. Alone in the field opposite the village is a solitary upright stone – Carn-na-Marbh (cairn of the dead), a perpetual reminder of the plagues of earlier centuries and a memorial to a very brave heroine of the time. The Black Death swept across Britain in the late fourteenth century and many people died in the glen. The churchyard became so full of bodies that it could hold no more, so an old woman conveyed them on a sledge pulled by a white horse to a mass grave in the field, which she then covered with a cairn. In later years the tall, flat-sided stone was erected to mark the spot.

In Fortingall churchyard grows the famous yew tree, believed to have been there for over 3,000 years, making it the oldest piece of living vegetation in Europe. When Thomas Pennant saw it in 1772 it measured 50ft (15m) in circumference and at that time the middle was much damaged, caused by fires being lit beneath its branches for Beltane ceremonies. The wood of yew trees was much prized in the past for making bows, yet despite the plundering and ravaging across the centuries the tree lives on and is protected by a walled enclosure beside the church.

The next hamlet the royal travellers passed through was Keltneyburn, crossing the stream of the same name before coming to Coshieville.

> *We then passed the village of Coshieville, and turned by the hill-road – up a very steep hill, with a burn flowing at the bottom, much wooded, reminding me of McInroy's burn – passed the ruins of the old castle of the Stewarts of Garth, and then came on a dreary wild moor – passing below Schiehallion, one of the high hills – and at the summit of the road came to a small loch, called Ceannairdiche.*

Coshieville was where officers of General Wade's building force were once housed. This section of the military road was constructed in 1730, forming an important part of the communication network from the north to Stirling and Glasgow. Many of the cattle droves came this way from Dalnacardoch, by way of crossing the Tummel on their way to the markets in the south. In the *14th Report to the Commissioners for Highland Roads and Bridges* in 1828 the route from Dalnacardoch to the valley of the Tay is referred to as the route by which go to Falkirk, Doune and other trysts 'almost all the cattle and sheep of the North and North-West Highlands.'

From Coshieville the military road climbs steeply, and within a mile Garth Castle can be seen over to the left. This was a lair of the Wolf of Badenoch, looking much today as it was in his time. It was an impregnable retreat for the Wolf and his followers, with its 60ft (18m) high square keep perched on an island in the Keltney Burn. The terror and punishment that he inflicted on his opponents is indicated by the following example: five men, bound hand and foot and blindfolded, were made to kneel opposite gaps in the ramparts; the tall figure of the Wolf then stepped forward and kicked out at the backs of his defenceless victims who jerked forward, tumbling to their deaths on the jagged rocks in the midst of the roaring torrents.

The road climbs for a further three miles to reach the watershed amidst open moorland, part of which is now covered with modern plantations. A prominent landmark is the Tomphubil limekiln, built in 1865. During the eighteenth and nineteenth centuries the large outcrop of limestone found here was quarried and taken to Strathtay, where it was rendered down in small kilns to produce fertiliser and mortar for building purposes. As the need for lime to improve both crops and pasture increased the large kiln was built here and remained in use until the early 1900s. A spectacular view of Schiehallion across Loch Kinardochy, a small fishing loch, was obtained here by the Queen. Schiehallion (Fairy Hill of the Caledons) at 3,547ft (1,082m) is the most striking feature of the area, forming a sharp cone and reckoned by many to be the most perfectly-shaped mountain in Scotland. The Caledons were an ancient tribe who held power in the area about 2,000 years ago. Schiehallion achieved fame of a different sort when the Rev Nevil Maskelyn, the Astronomer Royal, conducted experiments on it in 1772 to measure the density of the earth and there is a memorial to him beside the Braes of Foss car park. In his experiments he set up observation points on both sides of the mountain in order to measure by how much plumb lines were pulled out of the vertical and in towards the mountainside by the gravitational force due to its mass. It was also surveyed by Charles Hutton, a mathematician and a member of the Royal Observatory at Greenwich, who was the first to use land surface contour lines in his calculations, which are now universally employed in all map making.

Tummelside

Soon after this we turned down the hill again into woods, and came to Tummel Bridge, where we changed horses. Here were a few, but very few people, who I think from what Brown and Grant – who, as usual, were in attendance – said, recognised us, but behaved extremely well, and did not come near. This was at twenty minutes to four. We then turned as it were homewards, but had to make a good long circuit, and drove along the side of Loch Tummel, high above the loch, through birch wood, which grows along the hills much the same as about Birkhall. It is only three miles long. Here it was again very clear and bright. At the end of the loch, on a highish point called after me 'The Queen's View' – though I had not been there in 1844 – we got out and took tea. But this was a long and unsuccessful business; the fire would not burn, and a kettle would not boil. At length Brown ran off to a cottage and returned after some little while with a can full of hot water, but it was no longer boiling when it arrived, and the tea was not good. Then all had to be packed, and it made us very late.

The tea cup accidentally broken by Queen Victoria and some of the complete service which replaced it in 1866

Standing stones at Croftmoraig, seen by Queen Victoria in 1865

'. . . passing below Schiehallion, one of the high hills . . .' – Queen Victoria

Princess Louise, who wrote to Duchess Anne about the replacement service for Kindrogan

'. . . passed the ruins of the old castle of the Stewarts of Garth' – *Queen Victoria (1866)*

'. . . and I could now see the great improvements made at the Castle [Blair] . . .' – *Queen Victoria (1873)*

The Queen's View, Loch Tummel in Victoria's time

On the long descent to Tummelside Queen Victoria drove through an attractive area of natural open birch woodland called Daloist, now being managed as a conservation area. Within two miles she came to the River Tummel and crossed it by means of another fine example of a Wade bridge, built in 1730 under the supervision of John Stewart of the neighbouring estate of Kynachan. The building contract was dated 25 July 1730 and stated that:

Whereas it is agreed between Lieu^t. Genl. George Wade for and on account of His Majesty, and John Stewart of Canagan Esqr, That he the said John Stewart shall Build a Stone Bridge strengthen'd with a double Arch over the River of Tumble, within less than a mile west of the house of the said Canagan, which Bridge is to have an Arch of at least forty two feet between the Landstools (or more if the breadth of the River shall require an Arch of a larger dimension). It is likewise to be twelve foot in breadth including the Parrapet Walls, which Walls are to be three foot high above the Pavement, and at least one foot broad, and to be coped with good flag stones. The whole to be of good Materials and well wrought, and to have an Access to the same extending so far on both sides to the Land, as to render it easily passable for Wheel Carriage or Canon, And Likewise to make sufficient Buttments that shall confine the Water, to pass under the Arch, that in extraordinary Floods it may not damage or undermine the foundation, For which Bridge and all Materials, and Charges relating thereto, the said Lieu^t. General George Wade is to Pay to the said John Stewart, the Sum of two hundred pounds

Sterling viz: Fifty pounds on the signing this Contract, and one hundred and fifty pounds, as soon as the work is compleated, which he promises to finish before the last day of October next ensuing, and the said John Stewart does oblige himself to give sufficient Security before the last Payment is made to uphold the said Bridge at his own Expence for the space of twenty years from the Date hereof, . . .

John Stewart completed the bridge within the contract time, receiving his final payment on 2 October. Part of the agreement was that he was to maintain the bridge at his own expense for twenty years, and perhaps that explains why it still stands today, although now bypassed as being unsuitable for modern day-traffic.

The old inn, now converted into private houses, stands beside the bridge, and here the royal party changed to fresh horses provided by Fishers Hotel in Pitlochry. The inn was originally another base from which Wade supervised the road-building progress. The composer Felix Mendelssohn stayed here in 1828 when it was a single-storey building and he described his experience of it in a letter home:

. . . storm howls, rumbles and whistles outside, slams the door and opens the shutters. We sit quietly by the fire which I poke up at times, so that it flickers. The room is large and bare . . .

Queen's View

The homeward journey took the party along the north bank of Loch Tummel, considerably smaller then (before the twentieth-century raising of the level for hydro-electricity purposes), through natural birch woods skirting the water's edge to the Queen's View, which stands on a conspicuous knoll with commanding views over the loch and the mountains away to the west. There is no doubt that it was not named after Queen Victoria, as she herself admitted she had not been there before; but more likely after Queen Isabella, wife of Robert the Bruce, who had fled to the area for sanctuary in the early fourteenth century and traditionally hid nearby at Coillebrochan.

It was fast growing dark. We passed Alleine, Sir Robert Colquhoun's place, almost immediately after this, and then, at about half-past six, changed horses at the Bridge of Garry, near, or rather in the midst of, the Pass of Killiecrankie; but from the lateness of the hour and the dullness of the evening – for it was raining – we could see hardly anything.

After a less than satisfactory attempt at tea, they resumed their journey and very soon passed Allean House, now the Queen's View Hotel. As they approached the Garry Bridge in the Pass of Killiecrankie, the stark chimney gable of the old house of Coillebrochan might have been visible in the deepening evening gloom. It lies 200yd (183m) off the road and is reputed to be where Robert the Bruce, with a few of his exhausted and dispirited followers, sought refuge after the Battle of Methven in 1306.

Pitlochry in the 1860s

We went through Pitlochry, where we were recognised, but got quite quietly through, and reached Ballinluig, where the Duchess's horses were put on, at a little before half-past seven. Here the lamps were lit, and the good people had put two lighted candles in each window! They offered to bring 'Athole Brose,' which we, however, declined. The people pressed round the carriage, and one man brought a bull's-eye lantern which he turned upon me. But Brown, who kept quite close, put himself between me and the glare.

We ought to have been home in less than an hour from this time, but we had divers impediments – twice the plaid fell out and had to be picked up; and then the lamp which I had given to the Duchess, like the one our outrider carries, was lit, and the coachman who rode outrider, and who was not accustomed to use it, did not hold it rightly, so that it went out twice and had to be relit each time. So we only got home at a quarter to nine, and dined at twenty minutes past nine. But it was a very interesting day. We must have gone seventy-four miles.

Pitlochry had grown quite dramatically since the Queen had passed through it 22 years previously. While the Queen had set the fashion for holidays in the Highlands, it was her physician, Sir James Clark, who did much to promote the benefits of Pitlochry by extolling the virtues of its good clean air. Within a short time, wealthy families from the industrial cities were building houses to which they repaired for the summer months and the opening of the railway in the 1860s gave further impetus to its expansion, with the building of large hotels to cater for the ever-increasing influx of summer visitors.

That day Queen Victoria travelled over seventy miles on a journey that lasted for nearly eleven hours over the country's rough and bumpy roads. It was one of the longest day trips of her life and says much for her stamina and powers of endurance. It is another example of how she loved the wide open spaces, away from crowds – a fulfilment of her 'dream days'.

> *Thursday, October 4.*
>
> *Again heavy mist on the hills – most provoking – but without rain. The Duchess came to ask if I had any objection to the servants and gillies having a dance for two hours in the evening, to which I said certainly not, and that I would go to it myself. At a quarter to twelve I rode in the grounds with the Duchess, going round Bishop's Hill and up to the King's Seat, a good height, among the most splendid trees – beeches, oaks, Scotch firs, spruce – really quite like Windsor and reminding me of those fine trees at the Belvidere, and a good deal of Reinhardtsbrunn (in the forest of Thuringia). But though less heavy than the two preceeding mornings and quite dry, it was too hazy to see any distant hills, and Craig y Barns, that splendid, rocky, richly wooded hill overtopping the whole, only peeped through the mist occasionally. From the King's Seat we came down by the fort and upon the old 'Otter Hound Kennels,' where we saw Mrs Fisher, the mother of Agnes Brierly, who was formerly schoolmistress to the Lochnagar girls' school near Balmoral. We came in at a little after one, expecting it would clear and become much finer, instead of which it got darker and darker.*

In spite of the dull morning the Queen and Duchess Anne rode out just before midday for a tour of the Dunkeld grounds, which fit snugly in the relatively intimate environment of the natural valley through which the Tay flows. Their ride took them round Bishop's Hill near the cathedral and up to the King's Seat, a prominent tree-covered hill below the Craig a Barns cliff face. This was the site of a Pictish fort and a lookout for deer in the royal forest in the times when the early Scottish kings came on their hunting expeditions. They then descended to the Otter Hound Kennels built in 1849 on the site of the old Marshall Farm. Aeneas Rose, pipe major to the Atholl Highlanders, was master of the otter hounds at the time of the Queen's visit.

> *At twenty minutes to four drove with the Duchess, Miss MacGregor and Janie Ely following, to Loch Clunie by the Loch of the Lowes, and passed Laighwood Farm. We drove round the loch; saw and stopped to sketch the old castle of Clunie, on a little island in the loch, the property of Lord Airlie. The scenery is tame, but very pretty with much wood, which is now in great beauty from the change of the leaf. The distance was enveloped in mist, and, as we drove back towards Dunkeld by the Cupar Angus Road, it was quite like a thick Windsor fog, but perfectly dry.*
>
> *We stopped to take tea at Newtyle, a farm of the Duchess, about two miles*

> *from Dunkeld, where she has a small room, and which supplies turnips etc., for the*
> *fine dairy cows. We got home by five minutes to seven. We passed through the town,*
> *where the people appeared at their doors cheering, and the children made a great*
> *noise.*

Clunie Castle

In the afternoon the Queen and the Duchess in one carriage, followed by Miss MacGregor and Lady Ely in a second, set off on a drive which took them past the Loch of the Lowes and Laighwood Farm, the latter being one of the earliest possessions of the Atholl family, having been granted by King James III to John, the first Stewart Earl of Atholl, in March 1480. A further three miles brought the royal party to Clunie Loch, where the Queen stopped to sketch the loch and its island, an artificial lake dwelling on which were the ruins of a castle built by George Brown, Bishop of Dunkeld around 1500. The island was once a stronghold for bandits who terrorised the church tenants and in order to forestall and contain them, the Bishop built his castle and a chapel to St Katherine on it. His nephew, Robert Crichton, succeeded him in 1560 and, despite the Reformation, managed to preserve the Clunie lands for the cathedral. His son, James, who spent much of his childhood at Clunie Castle, was to bear the nickname of the 'Admirable' Crichton. At the age of twelve he passed his BA degree and two years later his MA. He was said to speak and write fluently in eleven languages, was a skilled swordsman and accomplished musician.

The homeward journey to Dunkeld was broken for a tea stop at Newtyle Farm, which was the property of the Duchess.

> *Dinner as before. At half-past ten we went down (through the lower passages) to the*
> *servants' hall, in which the little dance took place. All the Duchess's servants, the*
> *wives of the men-servants, the keepers, the wood-forester (J. McGregor, who has an*
> *extensive charge over all the woods on the Athole property), the gardener, and some*
> *five or six others who belong to my guard (eight people belonging to the Duchess or*
> *to the town, who take their turn of watching two by two at night), besides all our*
> *servants, were there; only Grant and two of the gillies did not appear, which vexed*
> *us; but the gillies had not any proper shoes, they said, and therefore did not come.*
> *Janie Ely came; also Mr Keir, and both were very active; General Grey looked in for*
> *a moment, as he was suffering severely from cold. The fiddlers played in very good*
> *time, and the dancing was very animated, and went on without ceasing. Louise and*
> *Arthur danced a good deal. Nothing but reels were danced. Even the Duchess's old*
> *French maid, Clarice, danced! She no longer acts as the Duchess's maid, but still*
> *lives near, in the adjacent so-called 'brick buildings'.*

That night a dance was held in the servants' hall at the Cottage for all the staff involved in the royal visit. Mr Patrick Small Keir proposed a toast to the Queen for her continuing good health and Princess Louise and Prince Arthur joined enthusiastically in the dancing.

Friday, October 5.

A brighter morning, though still hazy. The sun came out and the mist seemed dispersing. At twenty minutes to one started with the Duchess and Louise, the two ladies following, for Loch Ordie. Several times during the drive the mist regained its mastery, but then again the sun struggled through, blue sky appeared, and the mist seemed to roll away and the hills and woods to break through. We drove by Craig Lush and Butterstone Lochs, and then turned by the Riechip Burn – up a very steep hill, finely wooded, passing by Riechip and Raemore, two of the Duke of Athole's shooting lodges, both let. After the last the road opens upon a wild moor (or 'muir') for a short while, before entering the plantations and woods of Loch Ordie. Here quite close to the lodge, on the grass, we took luncheon. The Duchess had had a hot venison pie brought, which was very acceptable. The sun had come out, and it was delightfully warm, with a blue sky and bright lights, and we sat sketching for some time. The good people have made a cairn amongst the trees where we had tea last year.

This was Queen Victoria's last excursion in Highland Perthshire, when the two carriages set off past the Lochs of the Lowes on to Butterstone, where they drove off up a track to the left beside the Buckney Burn in the Den of Riechip – the burn of Riechip does not exist. This tour took them past the grounds of Riechip and Riemore, fairly late additions to the Atholl Estate, which have since been sold. Riechip became a shooting lodge, which in recent years was burnt down and is now a ruin, while Riemore is a private house. The prefix 'Rie' indicates that in the past both these places were shielings, or places of summer pasture, where women and children tended the animals and made their butter and cheese. The Santa Crux Well was beside the track to Loch Ordie, and a small chapel was built here for use by families in their shieling bothies. Many people came to the well at Beltane, believing its water could cure all their ailments.

There is a short stretch of open moorland as the track climbs the ridge beyond Riemore Lodge and descends to the shore of Loch Ordie, where a welcome lunch of hot venison pie prepared by Mrs McCall was waiting for the royal party. A substantial cairn to commemorate the Queen's visit the previous year had been built on the grassy bank overlooking the loch, and this obviously pleased the Queen.

At four we drove away, and went by the road which leads towards Tullymet, and out of the woods by Hardy's Lodge, near a bridge. We stopped at a very picturesque place, surrounded by woods and hills and little shiels, reminding me of the Laucha Grund at Reinhardtsbrunn. Opposite to this, on a place called Ruidh Reinich, or the 'ferny shieling', a fire was kindled, and we took our tea. We then drove back by the upper St Colme's Road, after which we drove through the town, up Bridge Street, and to the Market Cross, where a fountain is being erected in memory of the Duke. We went to see the dairy, and then came on foot at a quarter to seven. Rested on the sofa, as my head was bad; it got better, however, after dinner.

'. . . and to the Market Cross, where a fountain is being erected in memory of the Duke' – Queen Victoria

Their route then descended from Loch Ordie to Roor Lodge and then turned right on to the old upper Pitlochry road to take them to Tulliemet, on a high plateau overlooking the Tay, where tea was taken. The return journey took them back along the upper road past St Colme's and down to Dunkeld, where they drove through the town to the square so that the Queen could inspect the new fountain, erected by public subscription on the site of the old market cross in memory of the 6th Duke. It was designed by Mr Robertson, an architect in Perth and was inaugurated three weeks later by Duchess Anne. According to the *Dundee Advertiser* of 8 October:

> Her Majesty, it is believed, gave express orders to drive by this route in order that she might see the fountain with which she expressed herself highly pleased.

An eye witness described the fountain as being 'very chaste and ornate', but the *Dundee Advertiser* was less complimentary:

> It is without doubt a very happy and well pro-portioned design but for my part I regret that it is too much characterised by that Byzantinism so rampant just now in Cockneydom, and which Ruskin has done so much to foster. The genius of Gothic in this

country is identified with the clustered column, and not with the plain cylinder, such as is now being re-introduced. But the cylinders, being of polished granite, relieve the eye by their colour if not by their form and the light and shade of clustered shafts.

As soon as she returned to the Cottage the Queen sent for Mr Jack, a draper in Dunkeld, for a selection of his tartans and bought several lengths. Prince Arthur also went and visited two shops, owned by Mr Anderson and Mr Maclean and made some purchases.

Leaving Dunkeld

Saturday, October 6.

A beautiful, bright, clear morning, most provokingly so. After breakfast at half-past nine, we left, with real regret, the kind Duchess's hospitable house, where all breathes peace and harmony, and where it was so quiet and snug. It was a real holiday for me in my present sad life. Louise and the Duchess went with me; the others had gone on. Some of the principal people connected with the Duchess stood along the approach as we drove out.

Ironically, it was a beautiful October morning for the Queen's departure from Dunkeld and a crowd of some 300 people gathered in the cathedral grounds to see her leave. The Queen, dressed as usual in plain black with a widow's cap beneath her bonnet, drove off accompanied by Princess Louise and the Duchess, with Brown and Grant on the box as usual.

We went the usual way to Loch Ordie, and past the lodge, on to the east end of the loch, the latter part of the road being very rough and deep. Here we all mounted our ponies at half-past eleven, and proceeded on our journey. A cloudless sky, not a breath of wind, and the heat intense and sickening. We went along a sort of cart-road or track. The burn of Riechip runs out of this glen, through which we rode, and which really is very beautiful, under the shoulder of Benachallie. The shooting tenant of Raemore, a Mr Gordon, was out on the opposite side of the glen on a distant hill. We rode on through the woods; the day was very hazy. After a few miles the eastern shore of Loch Oishne was reached, and we also skirted Little Loch Oishne for a few hundred yards. We followed from here the same road which we had come on that pouring afternoon in going to Dunkeld last year, till at a quarter to one we reached the Kindrogan March. Here Mr Keir, his son and his keeper met us.

The plan was for Queen Victoria to take the hill road to Kindrogan, retracing much of the route she had taken to Dunkeld the previous year. They mounted ponies at Loch Ordie and rode to the Atholl boundary with the Kindrogan Estate, a little way beyond Lochan Oisinneach Beag, where Mr Patrick Small Keir with his son, William and Donald MacFarlane, his keeper, met them to take over as guides and escorts for the next stage of the journey.

Thence we rode by Glen Derby, a wild open glen with moors. Descending into it, the road was soft but quite safe, having been purposely cut and put in order by Mr Keir. We then ascended a steepish hill, after passing a shepherd's hut. Here Arthur and General Grey rode off to Kindrogan, young Mr Keir with them, whence they were to drive on in advance. As we descended, we came upon a splendid view of all the hills, and also of Glen Fernate, which is the way to Fealar.

Up until the eighteenth century Glen Derby was called Gleann Gennaid, local tradition connecting it with geese as it was a regular roosting place in the flights of wild flocks. In 1715 Lady Nairne changed the name as a token of her thanks to the Earl of Derby, who had intervened to spare the life of her son-in-law, Lord William Murray, fourth son of the 1st Marquis of Atholl. Lord and Lady Nairne built the Mains of Glen Derby at the head of the glen in 1722, enclosed it with a substantial stone wall and planted an orchard. It was accidentally burned down in 1744.

The route on this part of the journey was exceedingly rough, following an old track which crosses the ridge below Meall Reamhar to drop down to the Mains of Glenderby, two miles distant. The ascent out of the glen is steep, along a good track which now passes through a modern plantation, although it was open moorland in the 1860s. As the party descended towards Kindrogan they had a magnificent view across to Glen Fernate, through which the road to Fealar passes, fifteen miles distant, thus making it one of the remoter shooting lodges in Perthshire.

At half-past two we five ladies lunched on a heathery knoll, just above Mr Keir's wood, and were indeed glad to do so, as we were tired by the great heat. As soon as luncheon was over, we walked down through the wood a few hundred yards to where the carriage was. Here we took leave, with much regret of the dear kind Duchess and amiable Miss MacGregor, and got into the carriage at half-past three, stopping for a moment near Kindrogan to wish Mrs Keir and her family good-bye.

The five ladies – Queen Victoria, Princess Louise, Duchess Anne, Lady Ely and Miss MacGregor – were glad after their hot and tiring ride over the hill to sit down and have some lunch. Sadly, the exact spot is lost in modern plantations. Following lunch, farewells were made all round and the royal ladies set off in their carriage for Balmoral.

We drove on by Kirkmichael, and then some little way until we got into the road from Blairgowrie. The evening was quite splendid, the sky yellow and pink, and the distant hills coming out soft and blue, both behind and in front of us. We changed horses at the Spital, and about two miles beyond it – at a place called Loch-na-Braig – we stopped, and while Grant ran back to get from a small house some water in the kettle, we three, with Brown's help, scrambled over a low stone wall by the roadside, and lit a fire and prepared our tea. The kettle soon returned, and the hot tea was very welcome and refreshing.

The royal party drove on through Kirkmichael, famous a century earlier for its cattle market, which was one of the main ones in the country, often lasting for around a week and attended by people from miles around. Having driven up Glenshee, the Queen stopped at the Spittal for a change to fresh horses, soon afterwards pausing again by the roadside for a tea stop – this time a more successful one, with hot tea!

> *We then drove off again. The scenery was splendid till daylight gradually faded away, and then the hills looked grim and severe in the dusk. We cleared the Devil's Elbow well, however, before it was really dark, and then many stars came out, and we reached Balmoral in safety at half-past eight o'clock.*

Within a few days of her return to Balmoral, the Queen wrote to Duchess Anne to express her thanks for the time spent at Dunkeld:

> *. . . I am sure I shall look back on the days passed with you as my only real holiday and I am most grateful for it. My beloved husband blesses you I am sure from his abode of bliss for all the kindness, affection and direction shown to her to whom he devoted his whole life & so tenderly watched over . . .*

Among the other letters that Duchess Anne received from the Royal Family after their stay in Dunkeld was an interesting little note from Princess Louise, dated 19 October:

> *Dear Duchess,*
> *Mama wishes me to say she sends the teaset for Mrs Keir today. I am sure you will admire it. I think it lovely. I often think of my pleasant visit at Dunkeld and all the lovely scenery there . . .*

Thus ended a significant series of episodes, spanning over twenty years, in Queen Victoria's life. Though it was never very far from her thoughts, she never returned to Atholl, but did pass through it one day on the Highland Railway line to Kingussie.

Glimpses of Atholl

> *Visit to Inverlochy, 1873.*
> *Tuesday, September 9.*
>
> *At one we passed the really beautiful valley of Dunkeld, catching a glimpse of the cathedral and the lovely scenery around, which interested Beatrice very much, and made me think of my pleasant visits and excursions thence; then passed opposite St Colme's, the Duchess's farm, by Dalguise, and saw the large Celtic cross at Logierait, put up to the late Duke of Athole; then Pitlochry; after which we passed through the magnificent Pass of Killiecrankie, which we just skirted in our long drive by Loch Tay and Loch Tummel, in 1866. The dull leaden sky which overhung Dunkeld continued, and soon a white veil began to cover the hills, and slight rain came down.*

> *We passed close by Blair, which reminded me much of my sad visit there in 1863, when I came by this same line to visit the late Duke; and I could now see the great improvements made at the Castle. From here the railway (running almost parallel with the road by which **we** went so happily from Dalwhinnie the reverse way in 1861) passes Dalnaspidal Station – a very lonely spot – then up Drumouchter, with Loch Garry and Loch Ericht, fine and wild, but terribly desolate and devoid of woods and habitations, and so veiled by mist and now beating rain as to be seen to very little advantage. Next comes Dalwhinnie Station, near the inn where we slept in 1861 . . .*

As the countryside unfolded from the train windows, north of Dunkeld, Queen Victoria reminisced with Princess Beatrice over her past visits, each landmark evoking its own particular memory. At Blair she was able to glimpse the great changes at Blair Castle undertaken by the 7th Duke, who had carried out considerable alterations following the designs of Bryce, the Edinburgh architect, adding battlements and turrets in the Scottish baronial style to make it the castle we know today. This last journey through Highland Perthshire is like a microcosm of the many happy days she spent there, with little doubt that:

> *. . . these dream days in Atholl and Breadalbane were a perfume that sweetened her life to the very end.*

Bibliography

1. SOURCE MATERIAL

Charter Room, Blair Castle:

5.44   Atholl House – House Book, 1844.

7.443   Atholl Highlanders Record Book, 1842, 1844.

Trunk 61   Royal and miscellaneous correspondence.

Trunk 70   Forestry manuscripts including: *Woods and Forests as they were – as they are and in all probabilities as they will be*, 4th Duke of Atholl.

Trunk 75   Royal and miscellaneous correspondence.

Bundle 3   Correspondence concerning the application for the award of the Victoria Cross to Sergeant Donald MacBeath in 1858. Letters from Donald MacBeath to the Duke of Atholl applying to be taken into his service.

Bundle 9   Letters to Lord Glenlyon relating to the Royal Visit to Blair Castle in September 1844, mainly concerning household and sporting arrangements.

Bundle 26   Letters from John MacGregor.

Bundle 231   Notes on distribution of money by Prince Albert to the poor of Blair Atholl Parish and the Hillmen and servants in the castle, 1844.

Bundle 637   Diaries of Duchess Anne, 1840–46; daily entries as to personal and family activities.

Bundle 1330   Printed copy of the Act of Parliament allowing the Duke of Atholl to build a bridge over the River Tay at Dunkeld.

Bundle 1518   Diaries of Miss Amelia Murray MacGregor.

Bundle 1548   Papers relating to Queen Victoria's visits to Highland Perthshire, 1844, 1863, 1866.

Bundle 1549   Typewritten notes on the life of Sergeant MacBeath and his military career in the Crimea.

Scottish Record Office:

GD 1/53/97   *Contract with Mr Stewart of Canagan for a bridge over Tumble*, 27 July 1730.

2 ILLUSTRATION SOURCES

Blair Castle Collection:	Old photographs; portraits.
Charter Room, Blair Castle:	Sketches by Lady Emily Murray; maps; Royal letters.
Clan Donnachaidh Museum:	Old photographs.
The Illustrated London News:	September 14, 21, 28; October 5, 1844.
The Leisure Hour:	1 April 1868.
Royal Archives, Windsor Castle:	Old photographs.
Royal Library, Windsor Castle:	Sketches and paintings.
Mr Alasdair Steven, Old Ballechin, Strathtay:	*Queen Victoria in Scotland*, 1842.

3 MAPS

Charter Room, Blair Castle:

Plan of Atholl House, Gardens, Parks and Inclosures. James Dorret, 1758.

Dalnaspidal, Dalnacardoch, Upper Glen Garry. Eighteenth century.

Plan of Dunkeld in Perthshire belonging to His Grace the Duke of Atholl. Surveyed by James Stobie, 1780.

Counties of Perth and Clackmannan. James Stobie, 1783.

North East Quarter of Perthshire. Mr Stobie, copied by J. Stirton, 1815.

North West Perthshire. J. Douglas, 1821.

First Edition Ordnance Survey, Blair Atholl Parish, Dunkeld Parish, 1867.

4 PUBLICATIONS

Atholl, John, 7th Duke of. *Chronicles of the Atholl and Tullibardine Families*, Volumes I, IV, V, 1908.

Black, A & C, Publishers to the Queen. *Queen Victoria in Scotland*, 1842.

Coates, Henry. *A Perthshire Naturalist: Charles Macintosh of Inver*, 1923.

Constitutional & Perthshire Agricultural & General Advertiser, 1844, 1863, 1865.

Dingwall, Christopher. *The Falls of Bruar*, 1987.

Dixon, John. *Pitlochry Past and Present*, 1925.

Dow, F. D. *Cromwellian Scotland, 1651–60*, 1979.

Dundee Advertiser, 1866.

Fullarton, A & Co, Publishers. *The Imperial Gazetteer of Scotland*, c.1865.

Gillies, William Rev. *In Famed Breadalbane*, 1938.

Gordon, Seton. *Highways and Byways in the Central Highlands*, 1948.

Haldane, A. R. B. *The Drove Roads of Scotland*, 1968.

Helps, Arthur, Editor. *Leaves from the Journal of our Life in the Highlands*, 1868.

Hunter, Thomas. *Woods, Forests and Estates of Perthshire*, 1883.

Illustrated London News, 1842, 1844.

Jack, Thomas C. Publisher. *Ordnance Gazetteer of Scotland*, 1855.

Kennedy, James. *Folklore and Reminiscences of Strathtay and Grandtully*, 1927.

Kerr, John. *Transactions of the Gaelic Society of Inverness*, papers in Volumes XLIX, LI, LIII, LIV, LV.

Lauder, Sir Thomas Dick. *Memorial of the Royal Progress in Scotland*, 1843.

Longford, Elizabeth. *Victoria R I*, 1969.

MacMillan, Hugh Rev. *The Highland Tay*, 1901.

McLean, Charles. *Dunkeld, its Straths and Glens*, 1879.

Pennant, Thomas. *A Tour in Scotland*, 1769.

Perthshire Advertiser and Strathmore Journal, 1842, 1844, 1865, 1951.

Perthshire Courier, 1842, 1844.

Root, Margaret. *Dunkeld Cathedral*, 1973.

Saturday Post (Dundee), 1844.

Scrope, William. *The Art of Deer Stalking*, 1838.

Stewart, Elizabeth. *Dunkeld, an Ancient City*, 1926.

Statistical Account, Parish of Little Dunkeld, 1792.

Sun newspaper, 1844.

Surtees, Virginia. *Charlotte Canning*, 1975.

Victoria, R. *More Leaves from the Journal of a Life in the Highlands*, 1884.

Wheater, Hilary. *Kenmore and Loch Tay*, 1982.

Index